Elusive Justice

Elusive Justice
Beyond The Marshall Inquiry

essays by
Kjikeptin Alex Denny
james youngblood 'sakej' henderson
Joy Mannette
M.E.Turpel/Aki-Kwe
Bob Wall

edited by
Joy Mannette

Fernwood Publishing, Halifax

Copyright © 1992 by Joy Mannette

All rights reserved. No part of this book may be reproduced or transmitted in any form by any means without permission in writing from the publisher, except by a reviewer, who may quote brief passages in a review.

Copy editing: Brenda Conroy
Design and production: Beverley Rach
Printed and bound in Canada.

A publication of Fernwood Publishing.

Fernwood Publishing
Box 9409, Station A
Halifax, Nova Scotia
B3K 5S3

Canadian Cataloguing in Publication Data

Main entry under title:

Elusive Justice

       Includes bibliographical references.
       ISBN 1-895686-02-4

1. Royal Commission on the Donald Marshall, Jr., Prosecution (N.S.) 2. Criminal justice, Administration of -- Nova Scotia. 3. Discrimination in criminal justice administration -- Nova Scotia I. Mannette, Joy

KEN7970.E58 1992   345.716 05   C92-098578-5

• • •

All proceeds from the sale of **Elusive Justice** go to a special scholarship fund for Mi'kmaq students. The scholarship fund is called *the mi'kmawey*.

This book is dedicated to Junior Marshall;

through the Grandfather Spirits and the Creator
may you make for yourself
the mi'kmawey

Contents

Introduction
Joy Mannette
• 11 •

**Analyzing the Marshall Commission:
Why It Was Established and How It Functioned**
Bob Wall
• 13 •

**The Marshall Inquiry:
A View of the Legal Consciousness**
james youngblood 'sakej' henderson
• 35 •

**The Social Construction of Ethnic Containment:
The Royal Commission into the
Donald Marshall Jr. Prosecution**
Joy Mannette
• 63 •

**Further Travails of Canada's Human Rights Record:
The Marshall Case**
M.E. Turpel/Aki-Kwe
• 79 •

**Beyond the Marshall Inquiry:
An Alternative Mi'kmaq Worldview and Justice System**
Kjikeptin Alex Denny
• 103 •

The Contributors

Alex Denny is Kjikeptin (Grand Captain) of the Santé Mawi'omi Wijit Mi'kmaq (the Grand Council of the Mi'kmaq Nation). He lives the mi'kmawey[*] in Eskasoni, Nova Scotia.

james youngblood 'sakej' henderson is Chickasaw married into the Mi'kmaq tribal family through Marie Battiste. He is a lawyer, legal historian and treaty expert who serves as advisor to the Santé Mawi'omi Wijit Mi'kmaq. **sakej** teaches Aboriginal and Treaty Rights and Mi'kmaq History in Mi'kmaq Studies at the University College of Cape Breton in Sydney, Nova Scotia.

Joy Mannette is a sociologist whose area of expertise is in race/ethnic relations. **Joy** teaches race relations in sociology and Mi'kmaq Studies at the University College of Cape Breton in Sydney, Nova Scotia.

M. E. Turpel/Aki-Kwe is a Cree lawyer and professor of law at Dalhousie Law School in Halifax, Nova Scotia. Her areas of specialisation are international law and human rights. She is a member of the Indigenous Bar Association. **Aki-Kwe** is an auntie, sister, daughter, and friend — roles which she finds more important than her other titles.

Bob Wall is a writer and instructor at Holland College's School of Justice in Charlottetown, Prince Edward Island. During the Marshall Inquiry, he was hired by the Commission as a writer whose task it was to summarize daily events for the Commissioners.

---

[*] The Mi'kmaq way is a way of living organized around notions of correct tribal behaviour centred in family and communal relations.

Acknowledgements

I would like to thank Fernwood Publishing, in particular Beverley Rach and Brenda Conroy for their patience and creativity in editing and production. Errol Sharpe prodded me to do this collection and I'm glad he believed in it and in my ability to deliver.

Welalio'q to Mi'kmaq people who have given me the spirit to pursue this book. A special thanks to Patrick and Eleanor Johnson. I have learned much from you about how and when to use my power and/or give it away.

I hope that my son will come to understand that time spent on this work is an extension of my love for him and his father. This one is also for you, little man.

Introduction

During the Christmas season, I was working hard to finish the manuscript for this book. I had spent a particularly trying day, checking references and searching for the right words. I was tired when I got home. An hour or so later, I sat talking with Junior Marshall. He had come to my home, as he usually does at this time of year, to say hello. I was glad to see him. He was more well than I had seen him be in some time. We spoke of his father, the Kjisakamow (Grand Chief), who had died in August. We spoke of ice fishing and of David Milgaard and Robert Sylliboy. We spoke of his large and empty house near Whycocomough. We spoke of why it was that the next Kjisakamow would come from another family.[1]

It was as if I had conjured him up. I had struggled with the inevitable fictions that writing must entail and here he was. He lifted the Marshall Inquiry from the page and reminded me sharply of the human story it was. I believe that the spirits brought him to my home to remind me of what I should already know — whatever I might write, this is no fiction; it is real.

This book has been some time in coming. It began in the hot, crowded, airless St. Andrews Church basement in Sydney in September 1987. Newly arrived in Sydney, I too joined in the "best show in town" — the Marshall Inquiry.

Later that year, I met sakej henderson and Marie Battiste. They came to be very important in giving me a path to the Mi'kmaq* world. Through them, I came to know Kjikeptin Alex Denny. Through them, I came to know what Dan Christmas of the Union of Nova Scotia Indians has called the beauty and pain of Mi'kmaq life. I went beyond my "guides" and, like so many aglasiew (white people) before, I became lost in the pain and could not find the beauty. Slowly that has changed.

---

*Mi'kmaq means the Allied People. The Mi'kmaq Nation is a friendly alliance of many peoples who occupy what is known as Mi'kma'kik, or the land of friendship. This territory includes what are now known as Newfoundland, Nova Scotia, New Brunswick, Prince Edward Island, the Gaspé peninsula, Magdalene archipelago, and St. Pierre and Miquelon.

I continue to walk the outsider/insider tightrope and have located in myself a clearer purpose. I have learned from the Mi'kmaq to be less preoccupied with "noun-things." This has freed me to concentrate on process. I have been privileged by The People, who have shared in my joys and have not hesitated to tell me I was far, far from the mi'kmawey. I cannot live the mi'kmawey but I can learn from it. Today, the mi'kmawey is fragile and many seek to restore it to a fragmented and fragmenting world. That is part of the task of this book.

The essays speak for themselves with a clarity and vigour which I still find surprising. There was no "grand plan" in their assemblage; however, you will find a rare and intriguing line of fit. I am consciously resisting providing the reader with a "map" through which s/he may read them. That, too, would be very far from the mi'kmawey. Let me be obedient to my own culture, however, by saying this: Alex Denny, sakej henderson, Mary Ellen Turpel, Bob Wall, and myself have given you a way into the reality and the sham that was the Royal Commission on the Donald Marshall, Jr. Prosecution. The book is a collage of Native and non-Native interpretations; a collage also of writing conventions treasured, or defamed by the academic world.

The Commission did not provide justice; it did not even appear to do so. It did, however, change the way things work in Nova Scotia and for that alone I am grateful. Crucially, the Inquiry elevated to non-Native consciousness the spiritual bankruptcy of our world and the resiliency of Mi'kmaq tribal culture. Crucially, the Inquiry has presented a stinging indictment of what the dominant society has tried to do to Mi'kmaq People.

Joy Mannette
Sydney, Nova Scotia
December 1991

---

[1] Kjisakamow Donald Marshall Sr. died on August 25, 1991. Had events not intervened, it would have been customary for the position to be offered, by the Santé Mawi'omi Wijit Mi'kmaq, to his eldest son, "Junior" Marshall. Customarily, the person to whom the position is offered bears within him the characteristics of what the Mi'kmaq People consider to be the finest attributes of their culture. As a result of his experiences, Junior Marshall knows that his tribal ethos has been fractured and that he no longer bears within him the mi'kmawey necessary for the work of Kjisakamow. It is the hope of The People that Junior Marshall's spirit will be healed, so that he may live the mi'kmawey.

Analyzing the Marshall Commission: Why It was Established and How It Functioned
Bob Wall

Introduction

The Marshall Case has been widely reported in the press[1] and has been the subject of a popular book (Harris, 1986). Donald Marshall, Jr.'s wrongful conviction, imprisonment, eventual release, acquittal, and the role of the Nova Scotia criminal justice system in the affair were the subject of an inquiry named the Royal Commission on the Donald Marshall, Jr. Prosecution. The government of Nova Scotia appointed the Commission by an order in council dated October 28, 1986.[2] The Commissioners sat in public for the first time in Halifax on May 13, 1987 to hear arguments on the issue of funding for parties to the Inquiry.[3] Formal public hearings on the issues arising from the Marshall Case started in a church basement in Sydney, Nova Scotia, four months later and continued periodically for over a year.[4] In all, the Commission sat for ninety-three days in four locations, one in Sydney and three in Halifax. It heard from 112 witnesses, some of whom testified more than once, recorded more than 16,300 pages of transcript and received close to 200 lengthy documents into evidence.[5] Two matters raised at the hearings were appealed to the Supreme Court of Canada.[6] There has been limited scholarly investigation of the case, or of the circumstances, political, social, economic, or cultural, which brought about the establishment of the Royal Commission itself (see Mannette, 1988, 1990; Wall, 1988; 1989).

The seven-volume report of the Commission was released in January 1990. The failures of the criminal justice system in Nova Scotia were revealed in the wide-ranging inquiry conducted by the Royal Commission. The work of the Commission and the Marshall Case itself have had and will continue to have a significant effect on the administration of justice in Nova Scotia and elsewhere.[7]

To understand what effect the Royal Commission has had and may have in the future, it is important to look at the origins of the Commission.

Some obvious questions arise. Why was it established? Did it grow from a sincere desire on the part of the provincial government to understand what went wrong in the case of Donald Marshall, Jr.? Did the province wish to use the Marshall Case as a springboard for a broader look at the operations of the criminal justice system? Was it intended to find scapegoats and thereby protect the integrity of the system as a whole? Was it simply a public relations gesture to defuse criticism of the criminal justice system? Did the province believe, perhaps, that a royal commission would exonerate the system and confirm that Marshall himself was responsible for his own undoing as the 1982 Court of Appeals had concluded? Was it an attempt to restore racial hegemony as suggested by Mannette (1988)? Did it result from pressures within the justice community to reform itself? Was it forced upon a reluctant province and legal community by pressures from outside the system? Or was its establishment the result of some combination of these factors? We must also ask how we can understand this royal commission in the light of criminological theories about the relationship between individuals and the state in the context of the criminal justice system.

This article will try to answer these questions. I will begin by presenting a brief overview of the Marshall Case to point out the reasons why Junior Marshall was arrested, convicted and imprisoned for eleven years. I will then examine the period from Marshall's release until the announcement of the Royal Commission and show what factors may have caused the Commission to be established. The mandate of the Commission and how the Commissioners interpreted their mandate will also be explored. I will argue that the Commission resulted from a variety of external pressures on the provincial government; that the Commissioners expanded the limits of their mandate to serve their own purposes; and that the broadening of the mandate caused unintended results which, in turn, caused the provincial government to react. In conclusion, I suggest that the work of the Commission can be best explained by applying the theory of relative autonomy.

The Marshall Case[8]

The Incident
As far as I can establish, what follows are the "facts" of the Marshall Case. Donald Marshall, Jr. was with Sanford "Sandy" Seale in Wentworth Park in Sydney on the night of May 28, 1971. On Crescent Street, which borders the park they met two men, Roy Ebsary and Jimmy MacNeil. Ebsary stabbed Seale in the stomach. Ebsary slashed Marshall on the left forearm and Marshall ran off. Ebsary and MacNeil went to Ebsary's house which was nearby.

Seale was found by a couple on their way home from a dance at a local parish hall. Marshall, meanwhile, met a youth named Maynard Chant on the street across the park from the scene of the stabbing. He told Chant what had happened, then flagged down a car in which he and Chant returned to the scene. Police and an ambulance were called. Seale was taken to Sydney City Hospital in the ambulance. Marshall was taken to the hospital by the police. He received stitches to close his wound, gave a brief description of the assailants to the police and was allowed to go home. Police were unable to locate the assailants described by Marshall. They did locate and talk with Chant who told them how he came to be at the scene.

The Investigation

The following morning, Saturday May 29, 1971, John MacIntyre, Chief of Detectives of the Sydney City Police, took over the investigation. Seale died that evening. Marshall voluntarily spent all of Saturday and most of Sunday at the police station to be of assistance. On one of his trips back to the Membertou Reserve, where he lived, Marshall repeated his story to an acquaintance named John Pratico in front of Pratico's house near the police station. On Sunday afternoon, MacIntyre interviewed Chant who gave a statement saying that he had witnessed the stabbing. He described the scene as he had heard it from Marshall, adding a few embroidered details of his own creation. Marshall gave his formal statement to MacIntyre shortly afterwards. Pratico was then brought to the police station where he first denied being in the park on Friday night and then gave a statement saying he was there. He described the scene as related to him by Marshall, also adding a few imaginary details.[9]

The following Friday, MacIntyre re-interviewed Pratico who gave a statement saying that he had seen Marshall stab Seale. MacIntyre then re-interviewed Chant, reasoning that if Pratico had seen the stabbing, and Chant was also in the park as he had previously stated, he too must have seen the incident. Chant also gave a statement saying that he, too, had seen Marshall stab Seale. Although the statements contained a number of mutually contradictory assertions and there was no other evidence on which to base a charge, MacIntyre presented these "facts" to Crown Prosecutor, Donald C. MacNeil, and was authorized to obtain a warrant for Marshall on a charge of second degree murder. Marshall was arrested that evening and held in the county jail until his trial on November 2, 1971.

Between Marshall's arrest and trial, the only additional information of significance obtained by MacIntyre was a statement from fourteen-year-old Patricia Harris. She said that she had seen Marshall on Crescent

Street shortly before the incident. Her first statement to police said that Marshall was with two men whom she described in a manner similar to the description given by Marshall. A second statement asserted that Marshall and Seale were alone on Crescent Street when she saw them.

Legal Proceedings

The first statements of Pratico, Chant, and Harris, which tended to corroborate Marshall's account of the incident, were not used in the prosecution's case, and apparently were not known to the defence. Likewise, statements to police from others in the park which mentioned the two other men were not used by either the prosecution or the defence. The murder weapon was not found and no evidence of motive for the alleged stabbing was offered.

Marshall was tried before a judge and jury, convicted on the basis of the eye-witness testimony of the three teenagers, and sentenced to life-imprisonment on November 5, 1971. Within a few days of the conviction, Jimmy MacNeil came forward to police and said he had been in the park with a man named Roy Newman Ebsary on the night of the stabbing. MacNeil named Ebsary as the assailant of Sandy Seale. This information was not made known to lawyers for Marshall who were pressing an appeal at the time. A hasty RCMP investigation of the allegation made by MacNeil discounted his claim and Marshall's conviction was sustained on appeal in late November 1971.

Re-investigation

Marshall spent eleven years in prison, maintaining his innocence and pressing his friends to keep searching for the identity of the real murderer.[10] By chance in 1981, he learned the name of Ebsary from a friend and set in motion another investigation by the RCMP in 1982. The re-investigation of the case by the RCMP determined that Chant, Pratico, and Harris had given perjured testimony at Marshall's trial. They claimed that they gave their statements and testified as they did due to pressure from Detective MacIntyre. The re-investigation exonerated Marshall and resulted in a charge being brought against Ebsary on May 12, 1983.

Marshall was released on parole and subsequently granted bail while waiting for a special reference to the Nova Scotia Court of Appeals. The Appeal Court held that there was insufficient evidence to warrant a conviction of Marshall and found him not guilty. In its 1982 decision, however, the court ruled that no miscarriage of justice had occurred. They blamed Marshall for his own conviction because, they said, "he lied to police and his lawyers."

After three trials, in 1985 Roy Ebsary was convicted of manslaughter for killing Seale and sentenced to one year in the Cape Breton County Correctional Center.

Compensation

After a protracted period of wrangling between the Attorney General's Department and Marshall's lawyers, in August 1984 Marshall was awarded $270,000 in compensation for his eleven years in jail. From that amount he paid lawyers' fees of over $100,000. Following release of the Royal Commission Report in 1990, Marshall received additional compensation and his family was also compensated monetarily. The bizarre nature of the case resulted in pressure upon the government from the media, opposition political parties, and groups of citizens to set up an inquiry into the justice system in the province. Finally, in October 1986, seventeen years after Marshall's conviction and four years after he was exonerated, the provincial government established the Royal Commission on the Donald Marshall, Jr. Prosecution.[11]

Setting Up the Royal Commission

The decision to establish a royal commission was not made in haste. The RCMP investigation, which disclosed that critical testimony at Marshall's 1971 trial was perjured, took place in early 1982. More than four and a half years elapsed before the province agreed to a formal public look at the circumstances that gave rise to the perjured testimony. The 1982 Nova Scotia Court of Appeals, which heard the special reference that resulted in Marshall's acquittal, could also have elicited testimony about the police investigation and conduct of the trial but chose not to do so.[12] A one-person judicial inquiry established in March 1984 to make recommendations on the issue of compensation for Marshall indicated that it would explore this area but ended before it had the opportunity to do so (see below).

Opposition politicians, members of the media, Native and Black organizations, members of the legal community, and individual citizens called for a public scrutiny of the Marshall Case and the functioning of the criminal justice system in other matters. At one point, the federal government is reported to have threatened to hold its own inquiry if Nova Scotia did not institute one.

Over the course of the four and a half years, the province offered a variety of reasons why it could not, or would not, hold public hearings concerning the circumstances of Marshall's wrongful conviction and imprisonment. In 1982, the province asserted that the matter was the subject of ongoing investigation by the RCMP. In early 1983, it was awaiting the decision of the Court of Appeals. For the rest of 1983 and on to September 1986, the trials and appeals of Roy Newman Ebsary[13] were under way. In addition, Marshall had launched a civil suit for damages against the City of Sydney and specific police officers. This civil suit was occasionally cited by provincial officials as an impediment to a public inquiry. As well, in November 1983, Sydney Police Chief John MacIntyre launched a libel action against the CBC and freelance journalist Parker Barss Donham. MacIntyre was in charge of the original investigation and, in a radio broadcast, it was alleged that he pressured the three teenaged witnesses to commit the perjury which resulted in Marshall's conviction. The legal action by MacIntyre against the CBC and Barss Donham was expected to cover the same ground as would a public inquiry. The suggestion was raised that it would be prejudicial to conduct an inquiry while this suit was in progress.

After Marshall dropped his action against the City of Sydney and its police officers in January 1984, the province returned to its argument that Ebsary's ongoing appeals were a bar to a public inquiry. In the face of mounting public and private pressure, on March 5 1984, the province appointed a one person commission to examine the limited issue of compensation for Marshall who, by this time, had amassed almost $80,000 in legal fees in fighting for his freedom and pursing compensation. This commission, called the Campbell Commission after Justice Campbell of Prince Edward Island, was restricted to the issue of possible compensation for Marshall, rather than a broader look at all the circumstances of the case. The Campbell Commission never did hold hearings because Marshall's lawyers agreed to negotiate a settlement on the compensation issue with the province. When the compensation settlement was completed in August 1984, the calls for a public inquiry continued. MacIntyre dropped his suit in late 1985. Finally, when Ebsary's last appeal was denied in September 1986, the province announced that it would order an inquiry into the Marshall Case.

While all of the reasons cited by the provincial government for its long delay in instituting an investigation of the Marshall Case have an aura of reasonableness, beneath the surface they lack credibility. None of the three witnesses who committed perjury due to alleged pressure by Detective MacIntyre had any role in the investigation or prosecution of Roy Newman Ebsary. Nor were MacIntyre or other members of the Sydney Police essential to Ebsary's prosecution. The details of the Marshall investigation and the way the case was handled by the prosecution, the defence and the court were entirely separate and distinct from the Ebsary Case except for the fact that both were charged with the same crime. By 1982, it was clear that Marshall had not committed the offence and it is difficult to understand how a look at the circumstances of an eleven-year-old investigation and trial, already recognized as flawed, could have affected the Ebsary Case, except that it ruled out Marshall as the assailant, which was not an issue.

The claims that Marshall's civil suit against the City of Sydney and named police officers or that MacIntyre's libel action against journalists and the CBC might be affected by a public inquiry were undoubtedly true. Many of the same issues would arise in either of these suits as would be present in a public inquiry. However, here again the issues can be clearly distinguished. Neither civil suit afforded the scope to look beyond the specific issues at law, that is, whether there was misconduct on the part of the police in Marshall's suit, or whether the journalists libelled MacIntyre in their report. Moreover, where the public interest in the administration of justice is concerned, other cases, notably the Grange Inquiry into the infant deaths at the Sick Children's Hospital in Toronto, have been conducted while police were still involved in ongoing criminal investigations. Given the importance of the question of how the wrong man went through the system with all its alleged safeguards for the protection of the innocent and was convicted and imprisoned for eleven years, the province could, had it been interested in doing so, have convened an inquiry as soon as it determined that an error had been made.

From the time of Marshall's 1982 exoneration by the RCMP investigation, it was clear that compensation for the eleven years of wrongful imprisonment was a central concern for the province. An inquiry that might show misconduct on the part of agents and officials of the Attorney General's department of the province of Nova Scotia would enhance Marshall's claim for substantial damages for the wrongful imprisonment. This concern was never directly alluded to by provincial officials but the media speculated that this factor might be a reason for the delay. At first, provincial officials contended that compensation should be a federal responsibility. They argued that Marshall, as a Native person, was not the responsibility of the province; that he had been convicted of an offence against the Criminal Code of Canada in a court with a federally appointed judge; and that he had been incarcerated in a federal institution for most of the eleven years. This argument was quickly rejected by federal authorities who pointed out that the administration of justice is clearly a provincial responsibility.

The contention that the province was not responsible for compensation was just the first of a long list of excuses which the province offered for not airing the dirty laundry associated with the Marshall Case. Taken as a whole, the collection of specious assertions offered by the province makes it appear that the province wanted to avoid an inquiry or to delay it as long as possible. This leads to the conclusion that, initially at least, the Royal Commission did not grow from a sincere desire on the part of the provincial government to understand what went wrong in the Marshall Case, nor was it intended as a springboard for a broader look at the operations of the criminal justice system. It is equally apparent that the province did not believe that a royal commission would exonerate the system and support the 1982 contention of the Court of Appeals that "any miscarriage of justice was more apparent than real." Had any of these reasons been behind the province's decision to appoint the Commission, there would have been no reason to delay its establishment for years.

Aside from Marshall's own lawyers, there is no evidence of a call for a public inquiry on the part of the legal community. Steve Aronson, Marshall's lawyer for the 1982 reference to the Court of Appeals, testified before the Commission of Inquiry that the civil suit against the Sydney City Police was laid to exert some pressure for a public hearing.[14] Felix Cacchione[15] who succeeded Aronson and represented Marshall during the negotiations for compensation, used the occasion of the award to reiterate the need for a fuller public inquiry into the matter.

If the province's motivation for establishing the Commission was to find scapegoats and, thereby, to deflect criticism from the justice system as a whole and from the political system in which it was ensconced, it would have been more advantageous to start as early as possible and avoid the appearance that a cover-up or "stonewalling" was taking place. The longer the province delayed an airing of the causes of Marshall's situation, the more it appeared that the province itself and the entire justice system had something to hide. This appearance was meat for media speculation. From the moment in 1982 that it was learned the Marshall Case had been reopened by the RCMP, the media dogged the investigators, Crown Prosecutor, Attorney General, and Premier. The allegations of police misconduct, racist motives, interference by officials of the Attorney General's office, and a political cover-up were daily fare in the press.

Opposition politicians quickly raised the issue in the provincial legislature to embarrass the government ministers. Federal Liberals used the issue to discredit the provincial Tories and threatened to investigate the justice system of the province if local officials would not. Even Brian Mulroney, then running for the Pictou County seat vacated by Elmer MacKay, jumped on the bandwagon. He advocated a million dollars as compensation for Marshall and promised that he would push for an investigation of the matter if he were elected.

The Union of Nova Scotia Indians (UNSI), at odds with the provincial government over a number of other issues,[16] was understandably persistent in its calls for an investigation. The Black United Front (BUF), angered by this and other cases where it alleged that racism existed in the criminal justice system,[17] joined the list of organizations demanding an inquiry. Private citizens, angered by the situation, established a fund for compensation for Marshall. The discovery process for MacIntyre's civil suit against the CBC and the journalists provided additional information for stories in the media. And Ebsary's trials, appeals, and minimal sentence, compared to Marshall's eleven years of wrongful imprisonment, all added to the public outcry for an inquiry.

It is safe to conclude that the impetus for a public review of the Marshall Case resulted primarily from pressure exerted by the media, Mi'kmaq and Black organizations, private citizens, and opposition politicians both federal and provincial. However, by the time the government reluctantly agreed to allow a public airing of the case, the concerns being expressed went far beyond the details of one investigation that seemed to have gone wrong. The provincial government and the Attorney General's office were being accused of meddling in the affairs of the criminal justice system to cover up political wrongdoing. The justice system was being portrayed as overtly racist and was plagued by a growing list of alleged scandals involving ministers of the government. The announcement of a royal commission, then, can be seen as an attempt at damage control by the government. What was needed was a public relations gesture that would appear to deal with the problem. The Royal Commission on the Donald Marshall, Jr. Prosecution was intended as that gesture.

The Royal Commission and its Mandate

The Royal Commission on the Donald Marshall, Jr. Prosecution had a very limited mandate. It was set up to find out what happened in the case of Donald Marshall, Jr. The mandate directed the Commissioners very specifically to the events of May 28th-29th 1971 and what grew out of the events. The Commission was established,

> with power to inquire into, report your findings, and make recommendations to the Governor in Council respecting the investigation of the death of Sanford William Seale on the 28th-29th day of May, A.D., 1971; the charging and prosecution of Donald Marshall, Jr., with that death; the subsequent conviction and sentencing of Donald Marshall Jr., for the non-capital murder of Sanford William Seale for which he was subsequently found to be not guilty; and such related matters which the Commissioners consider relevant to the Inquiry;[18]

The Marshall Commission was asked to find out how things were done rather than why they happened the way they did. They were not mandated to find the motivation of the socio-economic conditions behind the treatment Marshall received. Nor were they ordered to look beyond this one case into the plethora of alleged incidents of political interference in the justice system. The Commission's job was to look at how the system had treated one individual and to suggest changes to the criminal justice system based on what went wrong in that single case.

The focus of the mandate is understandable in the light of liberal-progressive ideology which prevails in Nova Scotia today as it does in Canada generally (Silverman and Teevan, 1975; Linden, 1987; Chambliss et al., 1988). This ideology holds that the system is neutral or value-free. Justice is the blind woman holding the scales. If something goes wrong, then the proper response is to tinker with that part of the system which has broken down. By focusing attention on individual offenders, criticism of the broader aspects of the social structure surrounding the issue is deflected (Ratner, 1984). So, in this case, a mandate focusing on the specific problem of Marshall could be seen as averting attention from a general malaise in the justice system.

The mandate directed the Commission to inquire into four things. First, there was the investigation of the death of Sandy Seale. Since the investigation of the death was conducted by the Sydney City Police, this allowed the Commission to look at the how police functioned and, by extension, what it was that they investigated, namely the circumstances of the stabbing itself.

The second item was the charging and prosecution of Marshall with Seale's death. Under this heading, the Commission could examine the role of the Crown Prosecutor in reaching the decision to prosecute Marshall for the offence, what the charge would be, and how the prosecution was carried out in the courtroom. This implied, as well, scrutiny of the relationship of the Crown to the Sydney City Police and, in particular, to Detective Sergeant MacIntyre. In addition, the efforts of the defence lawyers could come under scrutiny. How they carried out their functions and their relationship to the police and prosecutor were central to the issue of charging and prosecuting Marshall.

Third, there was the subsequent conviction and sentencing. This permitted a look at the trial procedure; the evidence introduced; the testimony of the witnesses; the actions of the lawyers and judges; and the process by which the conviction was reached and the sentence imposed.

The fourth clause proved to be the kicker. "And such other related matters which the Commissioners consider relevant to the Inquiry." This gave the Commissioners the discretion to include or not to include a wide range of items. It is on this clause that an inquiry into the social system in general could have been justified if the Commissioners deemed such an investigation relevant to the Inquiry. Some would contend that the wording of the final clause was carte blanche for the Commissioners to range far and wide in their look at the justice system. Others, including the then Nova Scotia Attorney General, held that the phrase "relevant to the Inquiry" referred only to the justice system at the time and place of the specific offence and was limited by the construction of the first three clauses of the mandate.[19]

It is interesting to note some areas of the Marshall Case itself which were not specifically designated in the mandate. The mandate contains no reference to the appeal process; the jury selection and function; the subsequent RCMP investigations; the role of the Attorney General's office; the years spent by Marshall and his treatment while in prison; the manner in which compensation was awarded; the circumstances surrounding the reference to the Nova Scotia Court of Appeals; the treatment of Marshall subsequent to his release from Dorchester Penitentiary and prior to his exoneration by the Court of Appeals; or the issue of what role racism may have played in the Marshall Case.

The limited scope of this article precludes an examination of how the Commission chose to deal or not to deal with all of these issues and other broader aspects of public policy raised by the wrongful imprisonment of Donald Marshall, Jr. Some issues, such as the subsequent RCMP investigations and the role of the Attorney General's office were dealt with extensively by the Commission of Inquiry. Others, such as systemic discrimination in jury selection and the treatment of Marshall while in the custody of the federal prison system, received only a passing glance.[20] From the outset, however, it was apparent that the Commission did intend to look beyond the events of 1971. It was also apparent that the province wanted to keep the reins on the Commission.

The first skirmish was about who would pay for the lawyers of those given standing as parties to the Inquiry. Marshall hired prominent Toronto lawyer Clayton Ruby to represent him and then Attorney General Ron Giffin hinted that the province would not pay the $400 per hour fee that Ruby charged. Giffin suggested that the $175 paid to senior counsel among Halifax lawyers should be sufficient for Ruby as well (*Cape Breton Post*, Nov. 27, 1986). Giffin also implied that they would only pay for Marshall's counsel during the time that he was actually testifying and that the counsel employed by the Commission would adequately represent Marshall's interests at other times. A rash of newspaper articles and editorials suggested the problem was not money but a smokescreen by the province to prevent a full hearing of the details of the case. Giffin retreated and a May 1987 date was set for the start of the Inquiry.

Then other parties given standing by the Commission petitioned for payment of their lawyers' fees. Again the province said no. Terry Donahoe replaced Giffin as Attorney General and began what was to become a regular complaint; the Commission was going beyond its mandate and it was costing too much. "I believe the taxpayers of Nova Scotia are anxious to have that Commission get on with its work, *conduct the inquiry it was called upon to conduct* [my emphasis] and make its assessments and judgments" (*Cape Breton Post*, April 16, 1987). The Commission responded by announcing that the scheduled date in May would be used to hear arguments from the parties on the issue of payments for their lawyers. The Commission hinted that if the province would not pay so that the parties, as well as Marshall, were adequately represented, it would resign. Again, the province was forced back down.

In his opening statement at the May 1987 hearings, Commission Chair, Chief Justice Alexander Hickman, stated clearly that the Commission would go far beyond the inquiry it was called upon to conduct. "It is not enough to examine minutely one incident, and from that to expect to suggest changes within a complex system of administration of justice."[21] Of importance is the fact that the Royal Commission did decide to look beyond the specifics of the Marshall Case and to examine the justice system itself as well as the political arena.

The first hint of this was the Commission's request for the files in the Attorney General's office concerning two MLAs, Roland Thornhill and William "Billy Joe" MacLean.[22] Both had been publicly accused of wrongdoing involving finances but were exonerated by the Attorney General's office. Neither had gone to trial and, in both cases, allegations were made that the Attorney General's office had been directly involved in the decision not to prosecute.[23] The Commission sought the files to examine the treatment received by politicians and how it compared with the way in which ordinary citizens (for example, Marshall) were treated by the system. The question raised was whether there was a different standard of justice for politicians than for ordinary citizens. The Commission's decision to seek the politicians' files appeared to be an attempt to expose a general corruption in the administration of justice in the province. The province at first refused to release the files. It decried the request as a witch hunt that had nothing to do with the Marshall Case and, was again, a request which exceeded the mandate of the Commission.

Later in the course of the hearings, the province went to court to prevent the Commissioners from asking questions about Cabinet discussions concerning the Marshall Case. Nova Scotia Justice Glube ruled that the cabinet ministers must testify, but need not relate the specific details of who said what. The province appealed the decision. The appeal bench upheld Glube and the ministers trooped back to the stand.[24]

The Commission then sought to compel testimony from their judicial brethren of the Court of Appeals. When Justice Glube held that absolute immunity applied to the judges, the Commission carried their own appeal, joined by Marshall's lawyers, to the Supreme Court of Canada in a move that can only be described as shocking to the brethren of the bench.[25]

In essence, the Commissioners had taken the very limited mandate and, in the face of the obvious displeasure of provincial officials, proceeded to expand it to include a wide range of political and social issues never intended for scrutiny by the province. It was widely felt within the provincial bureaucracy and by political players that the Marshall Commission had become a "loose canon."

Conclusions

Neither the Marshall Case nor the Royal Commission set up to investigate it were independent of the society and culture in which they operated. Each was, and is, part of a complex process which began with a chance meeting of four individuals in a park in the City of Sydney, Nova Scotia, in May 1971. Trying to force the convoluted actions of the hundreds of individuals who acted in this drama over the years to fit a unified and coherent theory about the relationship of the state to individuals in the context of the criminal justice system is like trying to build a home of gelatin. As soon as you bring light to bear on any part of the construction, it begins to melt away. Only a theory that allows for change and flux in the complex array of interactions of individuals in society can account for the twisted path followed by the Marshall Case for nineteen years.

Marshall's arrest, trial, and conviction were the direct result of the incompetence of police, lawyers, judges, and other officials of the justice system that existed in Sydney in 1971, mixed with the bigotry and racial stereotyping typical at the time. "MacIntyre was the kind of policeman that the people wanted and needed at the time, a hard, no nonsense type who ran the city with a firm hand and kept things under control," said one lawyer connected with the Commission.[26] While from Marshall's perspective the system failed miserably, for most of the citizens of Sydney it worked to perfection: a clean solution to a very dirty incident with all the safeguards of the system observed and speedy justice prevailing.

When the RCMP re-investigation revealed that the system got the wrong man, belief in the integrity of the system remained firm. The misguided or perhaps vindictive actions of individuals were seen as the cause of the unfortunate plight of Donald Marshall. A quick admission that a mistake had been made followed by a sincere attempt to compensate Marshall in some meaningful way would have restored the veneer of legitimacy to the damaged surface of the system. Instead, the Appeals Court tried to blame the victim. The province, more concerned with keeping a lid on allegations of political misconduct within its own ranks than with the affairs of one Mi'kmaq from Cape Breton, paid scant attention to the sense of outrage that began to develop. Only when the province ran out of excuses, when it realized that further stonewalling would not silence the outcry, did it reluctantly agree to look into the matter.

The wording of the Commission's mandate and subsequent efforts to keep a tight rein on the Commission show that the province wished to keep the focus on the events of 1971 and on individuals who were "perhaps overzealous in their efforts to find a solution to a crime."[27] Even as the public hearing phase of the Commission was drawing to a close, former deputy Attorney General, Gordon Coles, asserted that Marshall's eventual release after eleven years in prison was proof that the mechanisms for protection of the innocent within the system worked well.[28] The actions of the province support Ratner's (1987) presumption that, when confronted with conflict, the state develops a political strategy to protect its own interests. One way to understand the process is to look at the manner in which the state tries to legitimate its activities. In this instance, the province, having failed to stifle the popular outcry about the handling of the Marshall Case, and fearful of close scrutiny of present-day practices of its criminal justice system, appointed a Royal Commission to examine an ancient and obviously flawed criminal investigation. The act of naming three distinguished judges from outside the province afforded an aura of legitimacy for whatever recommendations the Commission might make. If the Commission had stuck to its mandate, the province could have whitewashed itself by pointing to the changes in administration of justice that have evolved over the years. However, the three judges chosen for the Commission also needed to legitimate their own role and position.

"In order to develop meaningful recommendations," which it called the most important part of its mandate,[29] the Royal Commission defined its own agenda. The details of the Marshall Case "within the context of the current state of the administration of justice in Nova Scotia ... the role of the Attorney General as a member of cabinet in criminal prosecutions, the relationship between prosecutors, defence counsel and the police (both Provincial and RCMP) who make decisions to prosecute, and how and on what basis these decisions are made, the organization of police forces in

Nova Scotia, and how they interact with the communities they police"[30] became the new mandate set by the Marshall Commission.

If the Royal Commission had pursued only the mandate offered by the province, we might be forced to agree with those who, like Ericson (1987), view proposals for reform of the criminal justice system as illusions that mask the attempts of the state to retain and solidify social control. On the contrary, however, the Commission chose to exercise autonomy over its own affairs. This independence of spirit on the part of the Commission exemplifies, in a somewhat twisted way, the idea of Fattah (1987) who argues that attempts to intervene or bring about change may have an opposite result. The province appointed the Commission to defuse a growing crisis over the criminal justice system and ended up with a political time bomb that threatened to blow the government out of office.

Having lost the first two battles on funding and political files, the province was forced to resort to damage control. When the hearings revealed a woeful lack of training for police, a committee to study the issue was established. When complaints about the selective disclosure of information to defence lawyers by crown prosecutors were aired, a directive was issued requiring full disclosure. In anticipation of recommendations that the Attorney General's dual function as chief law officer and chief law enforcement officer be split, a new department of Solicitor General was created by the province. When interference in sensitive criminal cases involving politicians was disclosed, a special prosecutor for such cases was promised. When political meddling in the investigations of the RCMP was alleged, the Attorney General personally composed a letter exonerating the province of such behaviour for the signature of a retired RCMP officer. And periodically throughout the course of the hearings, the Attorney General sought to win public support for his fiscally responsible efforts to clamp down by floating exaggerated estimates of how much the Commission was costing the taxpayers of the province. When all else failed, the province took the Commission to court to limit the Inquiry.

What conclusions can we draw, then, about the relationship between individuals and the state from this brief look at the operations of the Royal Commission on the Donald Marshall, Jr. Prosecution and the reactions of the province of Nova Scotia which set it up? First of all, the Marshall Case shows that individuals and small groups, with patience, persistence, and a good cause can move the state to take action to address their concerns. Notwithstanding the fact that the action chosen by the province of Nova Scotia, in this case, may have been intended to placate those raising the issue rather than to correct the situation that precipitated the complaint, change has resulted. Whether that change is meaningful in the long term will depend on continued watchfulness and questioning of the actions of the state and its agents. If the province is allowed to slip the final report of the Commission on the shelf to collect dust, nothing of significance may happen and Ericson (1987) may have more fuel for his pessimism.

Second, the "relative autonomy of organizational components within the criminal justice system," (Ratner and McMullan, 1987: 109-110), especially the judicial branch which is seen as the most independent, can sometimes function against the immediate interests of other components. The judges of the Royal Commission carried their sense of autonomy and independence with them from the bench and rejected the attempt of the politicians to control their activity. Further, they called upon the other components of the system, police, prosecution, corrections (to a degree), and even fellow judges, to explain in public the criteria they used in the exercise of their discretion. The exercise of relative autonomy by members of the judiciary to explore other segments of the system can be viewed, ironically, as a warning that there are limits to discretion and that those exceeding the limits may have to account for their actions. This implies an "arena in which its [the state's] very autonomy can serve to promote democratization and reverse the class bias still evident throughout criminal justice" (Ratner and McMullan, 1987: 118).

While the final verdict on the Marshall Commission is not yet clearly in sight, it has already had an impact on the criminal justice system in Nova Scotia and across Canada as well. The successful attack on the principle of cabinet confidentiality alone is a significant change. The principle of absolute immunity of judges may be next on the list. At the very least, the work of the Commission has provided a wealth of information, not otherwise readily available, on the internal operations and decision-making of many legal and political actors — a scrutiny which has clearly thrown into confusion the sanctity of the justice system.

Notes

[1] The *Cape Breton Post* and *Halifax Chronicle Herald/Mail-Star* provided accounts of the original trial. The *Post, Herald/Mail-Star, Toronto Star and Globe and Mail* extensively covered the 1982 'Reference' to the Nova Scotia Court of Appeals and the reinvestigation leading up to it. The above plus the Halifax *Daily News* and numerous others by way of the Canadian Press Service carried daily accounts of the Royal Commission hearings.

[2] The order in council appointing the Royal Commission was given by the

Analysing the Marshall Inquiry

Honorable Alan R. Abraham, C.D., Lieutenant Governor of Nova Scotia, October 28, 1986.

3 Opening Statement, Justice Hickman, May 13, 1987.

4 The author of this paper was hired by the Commission to prepare a daily summary of the testimony for the benefit of the Commissioners and Commission Counsel. The task required attendance and substantial note taking during the hearings followed each day by intensive analysis to distill key issues of the testimony. Reference to these notes and daily summaries will appear throughout this article.

5 Closing Statement, Justice Hickman, Nov. 3, 1988 as reported in the *Halifax Chronicle Herald*, Nov. 4, 1988.

6 The Commissioners sought to compel testimony from the Nova Scotia appeal court judges who ruled that no miscarriage of justice occurred in the Marshall Case to find out how they arrived at that ruling. Lawyers for Marshall appealed a lower court decision that cabinet ministers do not have to testify about specific content and source of comments made about the Marshall Case during cabinet meetings. The appeals were denied by the Supreme Court of Canada.

7 One lawyer connected with the Royal Commission told me that at a meeting of attorneys general, a number of officials stated that they were watching the investigation closely and hoped to learn from it. They also expressed the opinion that they were glad it was happening in Nova Scotia and not in their own provinces. The results from similar inquiries in Alberta and Manitoba also bear scrutiny.

8 This summary account was compiled from testimony and documents introduced at the Commission hearings, newspaper accounts of the events (Harris, 1986), and personal interviews by the author with lawyers and principals during the course of the Commission hearings.

9 Pratico was known to the police as a person who hung out in the park with *Indians*. However, testimony at the hearings provided no insight into the reason why MacIntyre chose to bring Pratico in for questioning. In his first statement to police, Pratico said he was not in the park at the time of the incident. He first learned of the stabbing from his mother the following morning.

10 Of particular interest is the ten-year struggle of Roy Gould, Chief at Membertou in 1971 and editor of the Micmac News, to have Marshall's case reopened. He amassed several volumes of correspondence, the most poignant of which were from Junior Marshall himself as he tried to come to terms with life behind bars, while seeking to establish his innocence.

[11] The very name attached to the Royal Commission, that is, Donald Marshall Jr. Prosecution can be viewed as indicating the intent of the province to limit the scope of the inquiry to the details of the original prosecution of the case.

[12] Inquiry testimony by a federal Department of Justice official indicated that the focus of the reference to the Court of Appeals, agreed upon by federal, provincial, and Marshall's lawyers was changed after an intervention by Ian MacKeigan, the Chief Justice of the Nova Scotia Court of Appeals. See Rutherford testimony March 8, 1988.

[13] Ebsary's first trial ended on September 13, 1983 with a hung jury. The second trial resulted in a manslaughter conviction and Ebsary was sentenced on November 24, 1983 to five years in prison. Ten months later the conviction was overturned on appeal and a new trial ordered. The third trial also ended in a conviction on January 17, 1985 and Ebsary was given a sentence of three years. This conviction was upheld on appeal but the sentence was reduced to one year. A final appeal to the Supreme Court of Canada was denied in September 1986, one month before the announcement of the Royal Commission.

[14] Notes, Aronson testimony, March 14-15, 1988.

[15] Notes, Cacchione testimony, May 17-18, 1989.

[16] Notably the Simon Case which reached the Supreme Court of Canada and ruled that provincial restriction of hunting and fishing rights of Nova Scotia Mi'kmaq was superseded by the treaty rights established in the 1752 Treaty.

[17] Notably the 1985 Weymouth Falls Case where a white man was acquitted by an all-white jury in the shooting death of a Black man. See *Atlantic Insight*, April 1986.

[18] Terms of Reference of the Order in Council appointing the Royal Commission given by The Honorable Alan R. Abraham, C.D., Lieutenant Governor of Nova Scotia, October 28, 1986.

[19] "What is being looked at is the adminstration of justice in the province of Nova Scotia at the relevant time." AG Terry Donahoe quoted in the *Cape Breton Post*, April 15, 1987.

[20] When issues arose at the hearings that touched on federal jurisdiction (for example, parole or treatment of Marshall while in prison), lawyers for the Correctional Service of Canada raised objections, citing an unpublished agreement between them and Commission Counsel to restrict inquiry into areas of federal jurisdiction.

[21] Opening Statement, Justice Hickman, May 13, 1987.

22 Commission lawyers sought for four months to get the MacLean and Thornhill files from the Attorney General's office. (*Halifax Chronicle Herald* September 4, 1987) *John Buchanan: The Art of Political Survival* by Peter Kavanagh contains an interesting and informative analysis of the Thornhill and MacLean affairs.

23 Charges were laid against Roland Thornhill in 1990, a few days after he lost his bid for leadership of the Progressive Conservative Party in Nova Scotia. In December 1991, the Crown dropped the charges "for lack of evidence"; thus exonerating Thornhill after 12 years of controversy which has ironically now begun to ask if there is justice for the privileged in Nova Scotia.

24 Marshall's lawyers wanted to go further and ask about specifics; their appeal was overturned by the Supreme Court of Canada.

25 The Supreme Court overturned this appeal as well.

26 During the course of the Inquiry, I conducted formal interviews with ten lawyers who represented parties with standing. In order to secure their cooperation, I agreed to identify them only as "lawyers involved in the Royal Commission Inquiry" until after the Commission had completed its deliberations and filed its report. At this point, I have decided to have their contributions remain anonymous.

27 Notes, from testimony of Gordon Coles, former deputy Attorney General, June 21, 1988.

28 ibid.

29 Opening Statement, Justice Hickman, May 13, 1987.

30 ibid.

References

Brickey, Stephen and Elizabeth Cormack, eds. *The Social Basis of Law*. Toronto: Garamond Press, 1986.

Chambliss, William J. *Exploring Criminology*. New York: Macmillan Publishing Company, 1988.

Ericson, Richard V. and Patricia M. Baranek. *The Ordering of Justice: A Study of Accused Persons as Dependents in the Criminal Process*. Toronto: University of Toronto Press, 1982.

Ericson, Richard V. and Maeve W. McMahon. "Reforming the Police and Policing Reform" in R.S. Ratner and John L. McMullan, eds. *State Control Criminal Justice Politics in Canada*. Vancouver: UBC Press, 1987.

Fattah, Ezzat A. "Ideological Biases in the Evaluation of Criminal Justice Reform" in R.S. Ratner and John L. McMullan, eds. *State Control Criminal Justice Politics in Canada*. Vancouver: University of British Columbia Press, 1987.

Fleming, Thomas and L.A. Visano, eds. *Crime, Law and Deviance in Canada*. Toronto: Butterworth, 1983.

Garafalo, James. "Radical Criminology and Criminal Justice: Points of Divergence and Contact," *Crime and Social Justice*, Fall-Winter: 17-27, 1978.

Hall, Stuart and Phil Scranton. "Law, Class and Control" in Mike Fitzgerald et al.,eds. *Crime and Society*. London: Open University Press: 460-497, 1981.

Harris, Michael. *Justice Denied: The Law versus Donald Marshall*. Toronto: Macmillan, 1986.

Kavanagh, Peter. *John Buchanan: The Art of Political Survival*. Halifax: Formac Publishing, 1988.

Linden, Rick, ed. *Criminology: A Canadian Perspective*. Toronto: Holt Rinehart and Winston of Canada, Limited, 1987.

Mannette, J.A. "The Donald Marshall Inquiry: Everyday Culture and State Intervention," a paper presented in session, The Political Economy of Canadian Native Peoples. Canadian Sociology and Anthropology Association Annual Meetings, Learned Societies Conference, University of Windsor, May, 1988.

Mannette, J.A. "'Not being a part of the way things work': Tribal culture and systemic exclusion in the Donald Marshall Inquiry," *Canadian Review of Sociology and Anthropology*, 27 (4):505-530, 1990.

Notes, Papers, Exhibits and Transcripts from the Royal Commission on the Donald Marshall Jr. Prosecution. Sydney and Halifax, 1987-1988.

Quinney, Richard. "Crime and the Development of Capitalism," from *Class, State and Crime*. Longman: 31-62, 1977.

Ratner, R.S. "Inside the Liberal Boot: the Criminological Enterprise in Canada," from *Studies in Political Economy*, 13: 145-164, 1984.

Ratner, R.S. and John L. McMullan, eds. *State Control Criminal Justice Politics in Canada*. Vancouver: University of British Columbia Press, 1987.

Silverman R. and J. Teevan, eds. *Crime in Canadian Society*. Toronto: Butterworths, 1975.

Sumner, Colin. "Marxism and Deviancy Theory" in Paul Wiles, ed. *The Sociology of Crime and Delinquency in Britain*, Vol. 2, London: Martin Robertson: 159-174, 1976.

Taylor, Ian, Jock Young, and Paul Walton. "The New Conflict Theorists" from *The New Criminology*. London: Routledge and Kegan Paul, Chapter 8: 237-267, 1973.

—— ibid. "Conclusion," Chapter 9: 268-282.

Young, Jock. "Thinking Seriously About Crime: Some Models of Criminology," in Mike Fitzgerald et al., eds. *Crime and Society: Readings in History and Theory*. London: Open University Press, 1981.

Young, Jock. "Left Idealism, reformism and beyond: from new criminology to Marxism" in Bob Fine, Richard Kinsey et al., eds. *Capitalism and the Role of Law: from Deviancy Theory to Marxism*. Conference of Socialist Economists, London: Hutchinson University Library, 1979.

Wall, Bob. "Why Donald Marshall Jr. Spent Eleven Years in Jail: Reflections on Ethnocentrism in the Criminal Justice System of Nova Scotia" (unpublished). A paper presented in Seminar, Culture of Atlantic Canada, Saint Mary's University, 1988.

Wall, Bob. "Working in the Fog: The Marshall Commission Looks at Racism" (unpublished). A paper presented in Seminar, Culture of Atlantic Canada, Saint Mary's University, 1989.

The Marshall Inquiry:
A View of the Legal Consciousness
james youngblood 'sakej' henderson

Introduction
One night in Canada, a human killed another. A tragic event in time and space. More tragic, an innocent human was blamed for the crime and sentenced to life in public jails. More than a decade later, the actual killer was discovered, found guilty and spent one year in public jails. These simple facts evidenced a failure in the criminal justice system in Canada. To discover and recommend ways to prevent this failure to the Crown and Canadians was delegated to a Royal Commission on the Donald Marshall, Jr. Prosecution.

To understand the task of the Commission, a review of the structure of the criminal justice system in Canada is necessary. Under an express delegation of the Queen in Imperial Parliament in 1867, the federal government has the authority to state in general terms what sort of human conduct is prohibited in Canada. Canada enacts the prescriptive rules in the Criminal Code. The generality of the rules governing human conduct is important; it is associated with the political idea of formal equality before the law.

The generality of the criminal laws and formal equality before the law are two principles that reflect the artificial nature of an immigrant state. It is a voluntary association of individuals from various circumstances around the globe. To equalize individuals' social circumstances and perpetual struggle for their interest in comfort and honour, all individuals are viewed and treated by the law as fundamentally equal.

The general criminal laws enacted by the federal parliament are viewed as somehow above the antagonism of private interests. The rules are imperatives of the state. They are commands of an artificial political order over individuals, who have no inherent social or cultural order. By acts of a national institution the contending private interests are reconciled; rather than embody any factional interest in Canadian society, an impersonal criminal justice system is established.

Given the fact that the criminal laws are an artificial compromise between various interests in Canadian society, the greater is the importance of force and punishment as the bond among individuals to guide human conduct. Coercive enforcement takes the place of a natural community or culture. It is seen as the best way to guarantee order.

Due to coercive punishment attached to these ideal solutions to human behaviour by the national government, the criminal laws of Canada require uniformity of application to all individuals in Canada. The Queen in Imperial Parliament, however, did not delegate the administration of justice to the national government. Instead the administration of justice, by the Queen in Imperial Parliament, was granted to various local authorities.

The attorneys general and courts of the various provincial and territorial and municipal authorities apply the general federal laws to specific human conduct. To unite the different administrations of justice in Canada, the formal concept of reason is relied on as the fundamental technique of rule application. The adjudication process is one of the crown prosecutors choosing the best means to advance the ends of criminal law and to make specific deductions from the general rules; defence attorneys who challenge the prosecutors' decisions; and a hierarchy of courts and juries able to make conclusions about the proper application of the federal rules. The inherent diversity of rule application appears contradictory to the requirement of uniformity.

To unravel why an innocent human was convicted and there was eventual disparity of the punishment for the killing of the human in the administration of justice in Nova Scotia was the task of the Royal Commission on the Donald Marshall, Jr. Prosecution. Chief Justice T. Alexander Hickman was the Chair of the Commission. He was assisted by Associate Chief Justice Lawrence A. Poitras and the Honourable Gregory Thomas Evans. With the aid of many attorneys, the Marshall Inquiry was responsible for tracing and evaluating the decisions of the investigators, prosecutors, defence attorneys, juries, and courts under the federal criminal law to determine independently the correctness of Nova Scotia's actions.

If the law appliers in Nova Scotia could justify their actions to the Commissioners, the concept of the uniform application of the law would be upheld. If not, the uniform application could be rejected as a sham. If the law appliers cannot rationally justify their decisions according to established procedures, then those to whom the criminal law is applied are subjected to arbitrary exercise of local power. Legal justice becomes transparent; no decisions can be said to be uniformly applied.

Even if the law appliers would be justified in their actions, however, a deeper and more perplexing problem existed for the Inquiry into the facts. The human killed was a *Black* man; the innocent human who was convicted of the homicide was an *Indian* man; and the person who was guilty of the act was a *white* man. To determine whether the Nova Scotia administration of justice applied the laws correctly and uniformly, the Commissioners had to consider the purposes the criminal law serves in Canada.

In the different treatment of these persons for the death of a *Black* man, the *Indian* was punished for life; the *white* man for only a year. This raised the threshold issue of racism in the law appliers. The fact that an *Indian* was involved challenged the claim of legislative generality of the criminal law against the unique treaty relations his ancestors had established with the Crown. The Marshall Inquiry investigated the former issue and eventually had to confront the latter issue in discussing remedies to racism. Initially, the generality and the uniform application of the law in the criminal justice system were familiar enough to the legal consciousness, but their implications for Junior Marshall have been misunderstood. It is to these issues and how the Marshall Inquiry attempted to resolve these issues that this article is addressed.

The Inquiry[1] never clearly stated its methodology for determining the effect of racism in the criminal justice system. The legal consciousness is most comfortable with logical analysis and causal explanation but, in confronting racism and treaty rights, it had to confront the notion of unconscious structures in the human mind and artificial social orders imposed on Aboriginal peoples.

The *Indian* in Race Consciousness

Throughout the Inquiry, it was assumed by the legal consciousness that the race of a human was a known scientific fact. This assumption operated as a unstated common understanding. Race was perceived as an essential quality that marks a person's identity. There is no testimony that challenged this assumption during the Inquiry, either formally or indirectly. Yet, there is overwhelming evidence, biologically speaking, that no such thing as race exists. Every human being is a racial mixture. Humanity exhibits a continuum of physical characteristics, each physical type shading off into the next. Every conceivable nuance of darkness and lightness in skin colour could probably be found within the human race; thus, to single out a person as *Indian* on the basis of pigmentation has no scientific meaning.

While physical differences among people can easily be observed, the meaning of race is almost totally ideological. It varies among different cultures and different nations. For example, in South America, education, occupation, and income are dominant categories for classifying people. Race is a secondary category of identity. In Canadian thought, however, race is the primary status characteristic which sets *Indians* apart from others.

When one confronts the divergence between biological reality and social values, it becomes clear that racism is a social construct — a category of perception. In social science and law, race is an artificial way of classifying and identifying people. In Canada, it is not the colour of his or her skin; whether a person is an *Indian* depends more on what colour his or her parents are. What made Junior Marshall *Indian* was that the dominant society identified him as such. The Canadian perceptions are racist because they are made on the basis of circumstances beyond the control of the individual who falls under them.

It was obvious during the sworn testimony that most of the Inquiry participants assumed that race is a biological or anthropological fact. One of the purported eyewitnesses, whose testimony sent Junior Marshall to prison for life, stated that he did not know at the time of the alleged homicide that Marshall was an "Indian" [Chant 5/820, 991]. He realized this fact later when he looked closely at Marshall and saw Marshall's strong ethnic "Indian" features [6/1027]. Detective MacDonald, who had not previously known Marshall, stated that he recognized him as an "Indian" in the hospital [9/1633]. Roy Ebsary, the man who killed Sandy Seale with a knife, stated that he did not know Marshall was an "Indian" until 1982, but wanted to meet his mother, to see her face and judge her, and find out if Marshall was a "half-breed" [Ebsary 1/35; 2/355]. These statements illustrate the biological or physical anthropology bases for racial definition. Only the Mi'kmaq who spoke to the Inquiry discussed culture and linguistics as a primary status characteristic of identity.

The Inquiry, in my opinion, never confronted race as a social construct or a legal fiction. Race was an unalterable category that exists in the modern mind. It is the primary status characteristic in the legal consciousness of Canada. It is so dominant a perception in Canada, that there are no solid standards for determining when race should be a factor in the legal consciousness or when it should not be.

During its first week of sworn testimony, the Commission ruled that direct cross examination of the key witnesses about their attitudes about *Indians* was improper [Ebsary 2/358]. This prevented any authentic dialogue about racism. It prevented witnesses from sharing different experiences and knowledges, any thorough cross examination to reflect critically on racial beliefs and information. In such a dialogue, the Inquiry would have had the opportunity to build knowledge about racism in Nova Scotia. Preventing such a dialogue hampered the Commission and

Inquiry. It demonstrated that the Commission did not understand racism as either a social or judicial construct but, rather, treated it as a biological fact. This ruling by the Commissioners prevented any full examination into the hierarchies and ideals associated with racial perception in both the social and the judicial consciousness.

The Mi'kmaq as *Indians*

In the absence of critical examination of racial beliefs and information, the Inquiry validated the immigrants' view of the *Indian*. It accepted the racial tool of colonialism: the European invention of Aboriginal "reality" and their names for that reality. For example, not once did testimony of non-Mi'kmaq in the Inquiry ever mention the particular tribe of *Indians* to which Junior Marshall belonged. He was always considered an *Indian*, a member of a certain race of people, probably primitive in nature. There was no mention of nationality or ethnicity — only his race. Nationality, like ethnicity, is primarily a subjective phenomenon, a sense of social belonging reinforced by common language, culture, custom, heritage, and shared experience. The difference between being *Indian* and Mi'kmaq is the frontier between racial existence and being human.

Being an *Indian* is to accept the European colonial view of your racial inferiority. The continual use of the term *Indian*, usually as the equal of *nigger* and *coon* to Blacks [Ebsary 2/356-7; Carroll 49/9102], demonstrates the acceptance of colonial thought in Nova Scotian society and the legal profession. In direct testimony, the term "crazy Indian" was often used by Cape Breton residents [Pratico 12/2187]. The Sydney Police officers referred to Mi'kmaq as "Piutes" [A. McDonald 7/1255], "broken arrows," and "wagon burners" [Walsh 9/1467; E. MacNeil 15/2688-89]. In schools, the "white kids" used derogatory terms such as "redskin" or "squaws" [Gould 21/3732-33]. Such terms have always prevented the immigrant society from understanding the Mi'kmaq world.

The continual use of *Indian* by the Inquiry illustrated the legal profession's assumption of colonial thought. It perverted the perception of formal equality before the law in the legal consciousness. It raises the question of why race has became a key identifying category of tribal members in Canadian legal consciousness. Grand Captain Alex Denny of the Mi'kmaq Nation stated the issue clearly to the Inquiry, "You can't be the doctor if you are the disease."

At best, the Commission initially appeared to consider racism as a sociological problem. The examination of racism in the justice system was deferred until after the testimony phase of the Inquiry was almost completed. The Commission established a special study by Scott Clark on the Mi'kmaq in the criminal justice system as well as on Blacks in the criminal justice system.

Race Consciousness in the Marshall Inquiry

As the Commission began to acquire testimony and to search for understanding of the events which led to the conviction and imprisonment of Junior Marshall, racism appeared as the dominant explanatory principle for the failure of the rule of law. It was seen as the unity and the crisis of the criminal justice system. Due to the Commission's refusal to allow direct cross examination of racial attitudes or beliefs, the Inquiry had to deal with the racism through a maze of ambiguity of meaning and purposes.

To understand the effects of racism against *Indians*, the Inquiry typically relied on the actions of the key actors to derive meaning from the intent or purpose of the actors. It was clear that the key actors in the administration of justice in Nova Scotia would not directly admit to deliberate racial discrimination or prejudice. Such admission by members of the law enforcement or legal professions would be highly unlikely.

Discriminatory racial perception of humans can be approached in many ways. It can be evidenced as unconscious, indirect, unintentional, and systemic, as well as conscious, direct, intentional, and individual. Judge Cacchione's testimony illustrated one approach to the problem of racism. When he was asked about racism in the Nova Scotia criminal justice system, he stated that he believed that racism is present in Nova Scotia and, since the criminal justice system is made up of members of our society, there was a danger of racism in the administration of justice [65/11667-68]. This was an implicit statement that racism existed in the criminal justice system.

A converse alternative to this assumption, as the Union of Nova Scotia Indians' submission noted, to find that the criminal justice system is immune from racism, is unrealistic. There is nothing in the Inquiry to suggest that the legal consciousness operates any differently than does the social consciousness. Testimony showed that provincial judges, prosecutors, and policy-makers had never had any special training on cross-cultural perspectives [Matheson 28/5158; J.F. McDonald 28/5197; Lynk 40/7451-52]. The conventional wisdom was that the provincial criminal system did not need any seminars or workshops dealing with racism in the legal system or with the unique situation of an *Indian* before the courts [Matheson 27/5154-55]. Without training, the justice system could claim no special immunity from the dominant social consciousness.

The clearest admission of racism in the legal consciousness in the Inquiry was the advice given to Felix Cacchione from the Attorney General's Department. Cacchione was Marshall's attorney when, after his release from jail, Marshall sought compensation from Nova Scotia for wrongful imprisonment. Cacchione's testimony was that Robert Anderson, Director-Criminal in the Nova Scotia Attorney-General's Department, advised him, "Felix, don't put your balls in a vice over an Indian" [65/11673]. Anderson admitted to the Commission that, "it sounds like something I might say" [50/9155]; he said he thought it was acceptable practice to refer to the "type of person" a person was [50/9156]. Both of these lawyers are now criminal judges.

Faced with this dominant attitude in the legal consciousness of Nova Scotia and with no special training about racism and cross cultural issues in criminal justice, the Inquiry had to rely on indirect deduction about racism. The lawyers and witnesses before the Inquiry were aware of the prohibition of deliberate racial discrimination in the application of the criminal justice system; the Commission had to infer the scope of racism in the legal consciousness from the actors' circumstances and from the outcomes or effects of their behaviour.

The Inquiry's method of isolating the racism in action was thus defined by the intentions in an ideal or hypothetical manner (for example, what reasonable officials should have been thinking about and what they should have done). It was by contrasting the actions, or lack of action, of the criminal justice system and the results on Marshall, that racism was best defined. At times, in a particular situation, there existed a hazy line between racism and incompetence and negligence. Yet, nothing other than racism accounted for the systemic conduct of the provincial criminal justice system in Junior Marshall's case. The testimony reveals that the common racial conception that underlined the prosecution of Junior Marshall is one held by the dominant society rather than that acknowledged by Mi'kmaq people.

It was clear in the testimony that Junior Marshall was arrested and convicted because he was viewed as an *Indian* who attempted to assimilate into the dominant culture of Sydney and refused to accept a subordinate role assigned to him. In short, he did not "know his place." Law enforcement in Sydney was the protector of the dominant society, the enforcer of social etiquette.

The Union of Nova Scotia Indians' submission to the Royal Commission, prepared by Professor Bruce Wildsmith of Dalhousie Law School, concluded that,

> the overwhelming preponderance of evidence leads to the conclusion that the various checks and balances in the justice system would far more likely have worked for a non-Indian. Put bluntly, if any of the key actors in the justice system who touched his case

in the period 1971-1982 had fairly and competently applied their talents to whether Donald Marshall, Jr. was really guilty, the system had a chance of working. The fact that no one did and that the system failed had much to do with the fact that Mr. Marshall is a Micmac Indian (October 28, 1988:2).

In cruder terms, no one in the justice system was willing to put their "balls in a vice over an Indian," a member of a powerless, isolated race. It was not politically or socially wise for an attorney's career for him or her to challenge local or provincial authorities to protect this inferior human.

Race Consciousness in Sydney, Nova Scotia

Indirectly, the Inquiry addressed the field of consciousness, mind, or culture which existed in Sydney or Nova Scotia and the relationship between the Aboriginal peoples and the immigrants in Cape Breton and Nova Scotia. The testimony before the Inquiry demonstrated that a racist environment existed in 1971. Staff Wheaton of the RCMP testified that he had originally disagreed with the characterization of Sydney, Nova Scotia, as having a "redneck atmosphere." But after his investigation with a cross section of people (for example, educators, lawyers, doctors, merchants, and others) about racism in Sydney in 1971 [Wheaton 47/ 8590-92], he found that such an atmosphere existed and may have played on the jury's mind [Wheaton 47/7687, 8595-96]. When asked what he meant by "redneck," Wheaton stated that it connoted racial problems similar to those endured by the Blacks in the southern United States [Wheaton 47/7682].

The testimony also demonstrated that a racially stratified society existed in Sydney in 1971, at the time of Marshall's trial. The "Indians" were at the "bottom of the social totem pole" in Sydney [Ratchford 24/ 4463-64]. They were economically discriminated against. No "Indians" had ever worked up front in the stores of Sydney [Ratchford 22/4110]. Since 1958 to the present, no "Indian" has been employed on the Sydney Police department, or elected to city council between 1931-1988 [MacAskill 17/3068; Whalley 62/11232-33]. Between 1958-1988, no "Indian" had been employed by the city, as a secretary, fire fighter, or teacher [Whalley 62/11232-33, 11235] or practised law or worked in the courts in Cape Breton [62/11235-6].

The police regarded those "Indians" who hung around the public park as trouble-makers [Soltesz 19/3429; E. MacNeil 15/2634, 2665]. Youth were constantly being picked up by the police simply because they looked "Indian" and the police wanted to assert their authority [Gould 21/3883-84]. They were often told to "get back on the reservation . . .

A View of the Legal Consciousness 43

where you belong" [Christmas 23/4135-36]. Almost every week an "Indian kid" was picked up by the police [Cotie 18/314-95].

"White kids," especially women, who socialized with the "Indians" were discriminated against; it "was a no-no...in the public's eyes... there was a lot of prejudice at that time" [Soltesz 19/3350-51]. The police would tell "white girls with Indian boys to go home" [Christmas 23/4136]; often they reported these facts to the girls' parents [Csernyik 18/3278; Soltesz 19/3351; E. Clemens 19/3463]. Likewise, "white" people on the reserve were told to go home [Floyd 18/317].

In terms of modern social science, the Mi'kmaq who lived on Sydney's Membertou Reserve were alienated from the dominant society. The Inquiry testimony demonstrated the four characteristics of the alienation of the Membertou Mi'kmaq: powerlessness, meaninglessness, normlessness, and isolation [Burke 20/ 3600-05; Gould 21/3795; Francis 22/3900-05; Ratchford 245/4382-83, 4463-44; Aronson 55/10127-11129]. They were confined on the reserve on the edge of Sydney, detached from their old spirituality, detached from their traditional forms of work, and prohibited from any new creative or productive potential by the local people. They still retained a cultural and linguistic core [Francis 22/3926-36, 4082-84; Mollen 29/5429], but it was oppressed by all the local institutions, especially the schools [Cotie 18/3265; Gould 21/3732-33, 3738-9, 3785-86, 3847; Francis 22/3899-901] and courts [Francis/3918-19].

Continually, the local prosecutors and judges complained that the "Indian" youth "did not know their place" in society. The "Indians" did not belong in Sydney and merely came to upset the peace and quiet [Francis 22/3921]. It was alleged by a court worker that a local judge stated in court that a fence should be built around the Eskasoni Reserve so that "Indians" could not get out to come to Sydney to cause problems [Francis 22/3920-21, 13023-26, 4031-33; Mollen 29/5428; 2556; E. Gould 73/13021]. The judge in question cautiously admitted that he "may've made such a statement in jest or in frustration" [Matheson: 285157].

The sworn testimony presents the Mi'kmaq youth as warlike, "broken arrows" and "wagon burners" [Walsh 9/1467; E. MacNeil 15/2688-89]. Part of the reason Maynard Chant lied about being an eyewitness was his obsessive fear of "Indians" present at the trial [6/991-92, 1001, 1112-13], despite no evidence of contact, before the stabbing or after it, between the Mi'kmaq and Chant [Carroll 49/9108]. When Staff Wheaton asked Chief of Police MacIntyre why he thought Chant lied in the first instance, in addition to his personal fear of Junior Marshall, MacIntyre indicated Chant was afraid of "Indians" [41/7548, 7549, 7558].

In such testimony, it was clear that the criminal justice system and their witnesses defined their relationship to the Mi'kmaq in terms of unalterable categories of race which are connected with a certain image of the primitive savage. The belief which connects *Indians* with savages makes otherwise invidious discrimination appear reasonable. The belief's empirical falsity did not detract from its social force. Racial perceptions were imposed on social events. These perceptions, not the legal rights, were initial premises for legal deductions by the criminal justice system.

The cross examination before the Inquiry seldom followed up these particular expressions of value and belief. The attorneys did not seem to be aware of ideal-typical or structural methodological doctrine which could have provided a framework for exploring racism in the criminal justice system. This was unfortunate, since the actors' intent or purpose could be clarified if it could be isolated to biological, social, or legal constructs. This is the method adopted by modern thinkers from Kant to Freud, by Weber's sociology, Levi-Strauss' anthropology, and Chomsky's linguistics. This kind of social theory tries to unite the objective and subjective approach to meaning and to attribute universal tendencies or patterns to the unconscious of the observed.

No anthropological view of the Mi'kmaq culture, as contrasted with *Indian* people, was presented to the Commissioners. Yet, many witnesses commented on the cultural and linguistic problems of Aboriginal people before the criminal justice system and the perception of the legal consciousness of their behaviour. An understanding of this type of approach in the legal consciousness, in my opinion, would have allowed the Commission to grapple with the need to describe how and to explain why certain events succeed others, and would have prepared the Commission for better recommendations to the government of Nova Scotia.

The History of Immigrant Thought About *Indians*

Scant testimony or questions in the Inquiry addressed the causality between the surrounding environment or history of the Mi'kmaq and the Crown or relations with local immigrants. A former Attorney General of Nova Scotia stated,

> when we see an Indian person before the courts and in conflict with the law then what we're really looking at is the end result of centuries of discrimination and exploitation and a long, sad history ... that is just tragic in nature ... [W]hen we have native persons coming before the courts that's the end result of what has gone on for generations [Giffen 59/10735].

The history of discrimination and exploitation was ignored in the Marshall Inquiry. It was not seen by the members of the Inquiry as a general premise that explained how the criminal justice system came to validate racism in Nova Scotia. That was another methodological problem in the Inquiry.

The legal history of discrimination and exploitation, to this writer, is an alternative general premise which explains what has actually happened to the Mi'kmaq in the courts and why the Junior Marshall Case happened. It is equal to the assumed biological fact of racism, as a valid premise from which to postulate a growing string of consequences by logical deduction about the local criminal system.

The Inquiry ignored the problems which surrounded the attempts of Junior Marshall and others to integrate into Sydney society. While the testimony evidenced the stratified society and the police attitudes toward racial integration, the Inquiry never looked into the historical context of the public policy of assimilation. If it had, the Inquiry would have been better able to identify clearly the use of police and the courts in punishing those who attempted to integrate into Sydney's dominant society. If such an historical background had been explored, it is suggested that the activities of the local police would be seen not only as "redneck," but also as violations of federal policy and law.

The historic use of an undefined concept of the savage, racism and sometimes ethnicity, rather than nationality and treaty rights, justified the federal government's attempt to assimilate the Mi'kmaq into "British values," whatever that means. The introduction of social darwinism gave the federal government a practical theory of why the *Indians* had to be transformed in civilization. It stated that the *Indian* cultures are inferior to the immigrants' cultures. The federal government allowed the federal bureaucracy, under the Indian Act, rather than the general laws of Canada, to regulate every part of their lives.

Shortly after the introduction of social darwinism into British thought, it became the guiding principle of the federal bureaucracy in Canada. The bureaucracy sought to assimilate the Mi'kmaq toward British patterns of civilization. Part of Darwin's theory of natural selection — the idea of the survival of the fittest in the struggle for scarce resources — was appropriated to political thought by the Canadian parliament. Darwin's theory was taken in British thought to mean that "man" is the culmination of evolution, and that successful cultures were dominant because they were best and deserved to be dominant. Thus, the Canadian federal bureaucracy became the champion of assimilation of the individual *Indian* into provincial society through the destruction of tribal institutions of government. Tribal government and society were viewed as inferior to British patterns of government. Aboriginal and treaty rights were ignored.

Under the federal Indian Act, the designated Minister generally has the power to define for legal purposes who is an "Indian" (Sec. 5-17). *Indian* became the term that emphasized race and excluded them from equal participation in Canada. Until thirty years ago, the Department of Indian Affairs reclassified certain individuals involuntarily as non-*Indians*, automatically giving them formal equality with the immigrants. This enfranchisement policy, so-called because in many provinces it was a condition of acquiring the right to vote and participate in public life, was forced upon educated Mi'kmaq, and those seeking employment off the reserves, as well as those enlisted in the Canadian Armed Forces. Additionally, the Indian Act provided that a Mi'kmaw woman, by marrying a non-"Indian" man, irrevocably lost her status as an "Indian."

The practical effect of this racist definition of *Indians* was a subtle attempt to undermine tribal society, legally, politically, and culturally. This was not a hidden purpose; it was candidly explained by Canada's Deputy Superintendent-General of Indian Affairs in 1920: "Our goal is to continue until there is not a single Indian in Canada that has not been absorbed into the body politic and there is no Indian question and no Indian Department, (and) that is the whole object of the `Indian Act'" (PAC R610 6810/47203/7).

The segregation of the Mi'kmaq on the reserves appeared late in Canadian history—in the 1940's. While formal reservation of land for the Mi'kmaq began in 1763, segregation did not begin until the centralization era during World War II. Prior to that time, the Mi'kmaq continued their traditional migratory pattern throughout Mi'kma'kik. The centralization policy was developed and implemented while our men were fighting against totalitarianism in Europe. This "first social experiment of its kind in Canada" sought to segregate the Mi'kmaq on two reserves in Nova Scotia, Shubenacadie on the mainland and Eskasoni in Cape Breton. Then, the Department of Indian Affairs implemented policy to terminate Mi'kmaq special rights and political status, both with the object of another kind of involuntary assimilation.

To enforce the centralization policy, in a Treasury Board Minute, the Department of Indian Affairs introduced the Criminal Code to the Mi'kmaq. The Criminal law forced the Mi'kmaq onto the two reserves. In April 1947, Eskasoni's entire male workforce went on strike: for a wage of fifty cents per hour for ordinary labour, the removal of white labourers from the Reserve and increased financial support from the federal government. The instigator of the strike was convicted of "intimidation" under the Criminal Code. The RCMP forced the Mi'kmaq to go back to work at the previous rate of forty cents an hour, the 1942 rate. The coercive enforcements of the federal criminal law were used to implement the assimilation policy.

To accelerate the civilization and political socialization process, the Department of Indian Affairs removed Mi'kmaq children against their parents' will to residential schools which were managed by public or private organizations. At these residential schools, Mi'kmaq children were imprisoned like convicts, beaten for speaking their own language, and often forbidden to communicate with their families. Three generations were embittered and all family unity was destroyed by this "experiment in rural sociology" program.

The Department's "experiment" created instantly overcrowded ghettos with abject poverty and family conflicts. When the Mi'kmaq veterans of World War II returned home, they began to fight against centralization. A brief from eight veterans asked the Department: "When we were fighting for freedom against the powers of dictatorship, when we defended our country in its hour of need; did we think our own country would deny us the very personal right to live where we wanted to? ... Do the people of Canada believe we love our homes less than the Poles, the French and the Russians ... ?"

Faced with these problems, beginning in 1949, the Department of Indian Affairs ceased its centralization policy and began its policy of assimilation into provincial society. This is the operational policy under which Junior Marshall and his peers were raised. To facilitate the merger of Mi'kmaq communities into Nova Scotian society, the Department of Indian Affairs unilaterally created twelve artificial Indian Act Band Chiefs and Councils in 1960 and sought to terminate the traditional authority of the Grand Council of the Mi'kmaq Nation (Santé Mawi'omi wijit Mi'kmaq).

In 1957, the community development officer from the Extension Department of St. Francis Xavier University began working with the *Indian* reserves. The Extension Department documented the "sub-human existence" created by centralization. "Heavy drinking, constant brawling, sexual promiscuity, and many uncared for children," they wrote, "were the outward marks of their bitter frustration." The Department had created the "culture of poverty." Approximately 98 percent of the households at Eskasoni and 78 percent of those at Shubenacadie were receiving welfare. The RCMP and the Criminal Code became necessary to preserve order on the reserves; most of the time, the Indian Agent acted as judge; in some cases, the provincial courts became involved.

In 1969, the federal government finally sought officially to terminate the special legal and political status of *Indians* and assimilate the *Indian*. In its 1969 White Paper, the federal government's implicit policy became explicit. The government argued that "equality," or "non-discrimination" as it was often phrased, was the key ingredient in a solution to the problems of *Indians*, and that their special rights had been the major cause of their poverty and resulting problems (DIAND 1969). The goal of equality was to be achieved by terminating the Aboriginal and treaty rights and the bureaucracy that had been developed to protect those rights, and by transferring to the provinces the responsibility for administering services to *Indians*. In the future, *Indian* people would receive the same services from the same sources as other Canadians after a transitional period in which enriched programs of economic development were to be offered. By implication, the result of the policy would see *Indians* with "*Indian* problems" become provincial citizens with regular citizens' problems.

The White Paper's policy was essentially one of "formal equality," to use Cairns' phrase from the Hawthorn Report (1966), but the question remained as to whether it would foster equality of opportunity for this oppressed and disadvantaged minority. Three years prior to the White Paper, the Hawthorn Report had concluded that, "the equal treatment in law and services of a people who at the present time do not have equal competitive capacities will not suffice for the attainment of substantial socio-economic equality" (1966: 392).

It was into this policy context that Junior Marshall and other Mi'kmaq youth began meeting other youths in public schools and the public park in Sydney. The federal government's assimilative policy was affirmatively prevented by the local police. Contrary to this policy, the police sought to put the isolated "Indian" on their reserves, to "put them in their place." Numerous witnesses before the Marshall Inquiry firmly acknowledged that the Chief of Police was racist [E. Clemens 19/3463, 3515-18; Wheaton 42; 7687-88, 8604; Cacchione 65/11669; Gould 73/13048-51] and that he "was after the Indians" [Francis 22/4091; Christmas 23/4227].

It appeared from the sworn testimony and the actions of the police, that they saw it as their job to maintain racial separation, not to promote integration. They were never asked whether they understood that the federal government's policy was to promote the integration of Mi'kmaq into provincial society. It was unfortunate that the actions of the police to Mi'kmaq integration under federal policy were not analyzed. In studies of other "redneck" systems, it is common for the police to see their law and order functions associated with a particular racial order.

The evidence shows that same attitude allowed the police to fabricate eyewitness testimony and evidence to rid the town of *Indian* trouble makers — Tom Christmas, Junior Marshall, and others. It was not the first attempt of the local police to put the assimilating Mi'kmaq in prison. The police first sought to charge Junior Marshall with giving liquor to a minor

[Cotie 18/3247] and with knocking over the MacIntyres' gravestone [Christmas 23/4138-39].

Maintaining the social (that is, racial) order could have explained many of the administrative quandaries in the Marshall Case. First, we have the fact that the local police refused RCMP assistance on the murder case in which Junior was convicted [Wood 10/1820; 1825-27]. This was the only time that the Deputy Police Chief remembers that the RCMP was not brought into an investigation [MacAskill 17/3067]. Secondly, the Chief of Police spread a racial war story among the police. He stated that "the Negro community was going to take out their vengeance on the Indians and the Indians were going to take out their vengeance on the whites, who were lying against Marshall" [Wheaton 43/7884, 8603]. It is possible that creating this state of fear is exactly the Chief of Police's idea of how to stop the integration of Sydney society — since the morning following the stabbing, the Chief of Police, without evidence, considered Marshall a suspect [Wood 10/1820-03, 1821, 1824-5; M.B. MacDonald 10/1673, 1685, 1687]. Third, Tom Christmas was charged with obstructing justice to keep him from testifying. Fourth, contrary evidence was continually suppressed (for example, Pratico's confession; the 1971 investigation of RCMP Inspector A. Marshall of Jimmy MacNeil's confession that Roy Ebsary was the actual killer, during Marshall's appeals; and Donna Ebsary's confirming statements in 1974 that her father had killed Sandy Seale).

By November 1971, by the original trial of Junior Marshall, the White Paper was formally withdrawn by the federal government, and the era of self-determination began. The trial attorney for Marshall summarized the conviction that, "the jury must have said to itself, `He's an Indian and most likely he would've done it. He's a bad Indian ... He probably did commit it'" [Khattar 25/4576]. Marshall "had the burden of being an Indian" [Khattar 26/4888]. The interrelations between federal public policy and local actions, however, were not explored in the formal testimony before the Marshall Inquiry.

Mi'kmaq Legal Status

Without an historical understanding of how the Crown's agreement with the Mi'kmaq Nation had been undermined by centuries of discrimination, the testimony and formal studies of the Marshall Inquiry tended to degenerate into race classification as the exclusive premise of an Aboriginal person's identity before the courts. Thus, instead of legal rights and public policy, race became their overriding principle of social and legal organization. Colour of the skin, rather than treaty rights and obligations, became the criterion of a rigid set of expectations, equating white with civilization and brown with savages.

The Inquiry never confronted Junior Marshall's nationality. The implicit assumption was that his birth was racial, not involving any Aboriginal nationality. The fact that Junior Marshall was the son the Grand Chief of the Mi'kmaq Nation would have raised to anthropologists and legal historians certain cultural and legal problems. These issues of consensual politics are distinct from the voluntary people who have immigrated to Canada. It was only after the testimony was complete that recommendations of both the Grand Council of the Mi'kmaq Nation and the Union of Nova Scotia Indians were raised. These included the concept of tribal courts administering justice for Mi'kmaq on lands reserved for them by the Crown, rather than the province.

The assimilation era ended in 1973. On the 5th of July, the Queen assured the Mi'kmaq leaders of 1973 that, "my Government of Canada recognizes the importance of full compliance with the spirit and terms of your Treaties." With the Queen's assurances, the tribal self-determination and restoration of Aboriginal and treaty rights movement began. The movement successfully ended in Article 35 of the Constitution Act, 1982.

By ignoring the legal rights of the Mi'kmaq Nation, the Inquiry avoided the vexing quandaries surrounding the application of the Criminal Code to the collective treaty rights. The prerogative Treaties challenge the generality of the Criminal Code. They suggest that the federal parliament's artificial order does embody a factional cultural bias when applied to the Mi'kmaq. Moreover, they suggest that the federal prescriptive rules are not based on consensus of all Canadians, as Aboriginal nations and tribes have been historically excluded in the debate and their special prerogative rights ignored by the federal government. It also demonstrates that uniformity of application has an inherent bias against Aboriginal or treaty rights. Moreover, the specific terms of the Treaties directly challenge the alleged relations of individuals to groups in the modern theory of government and law. By using race, these deeper problems can be, and have been, systematically ignored.

The theoretical generalization of government and law behind the validity of the Criminal Code is inconsistent with the terms of the particular agreement of the Crown and the Mi'kmaq Nation in 1752-1763. Although ambiguities still remain in abundance, the seminal premise of the relationship was that, prior to European colonization and settlement of Mi'kma'kik, the Grand Council possessed full jurisdiction over their national territory and their allied people.

In the prerogative Treaties, the Grand Council agreed to delegate certain rights to the Crown, while retaining most of its preexisting rights. Except for those rights expressly delegated to the Crown, the Grand Council retains its ancient jurisdiction. In the Elekewaki (In the King's

House) Compact of 1752, the British Crown made it totally clear to the Mi'kmaq that their treaty rights not only protected and preserved their ancient institutions and cultural values but were also legally enforceable obligations in British law. The Compact is part of the documents comprising the constitution of the United Kingdom.

The prerogative Agreement placed the Aboriginal territory of the Mi'kmaq Nation directly under the British Crown. It did not, however, make any explicit delegation of criminal jurisdiction to the Crown over the Mi'kmaq. It appears to be unique among prerogative Treaties with the American nations. Instead, the Compact clearly established His Majesty's civil law as the guardian of Aboriginal and treaty rights. The mutually agreed upon procedure for protecting these rights was provided in Article 8 of the Compact. Article 8 stated,

> That all Disputes whatsoever that may happen to arise between the Indians now at Peace and others[,] shall be tried in His Majesty Courts of Civil Judicature, where the Indians shall have the same benefits, Advantages & Privileges of any other of His Majesty's Subjects.

Article 5 of the various accession Treaties of the Hunting Districts of the Grand Council to the Compact confirmed this principle that the Mi'kmaq "will apply for redress according to the Laws established in His said Majesty's Dominions (C) 217/18/276; PANS MSS Doc. Vol. 27, No. 14).

Article 8 mandated the judiciary to protect the Mi'kmaq under the Rule of Law. Interpreting Article 8 of the Compact and Article V of the accession Treaties, in 1761, the first Chief Justice in Canada, Jonathan Belcher, who was also President of His Majesty's Council and Commander-in Chief of the Province, stated that Treaties created a legal "Wall" and "Hedge" between the Mi'kmaq and the British settlers. This jurisdictional wall safeguarded the Mi'kmaq from the political and economic actions of the British immigrants; this wall was the British rule of law. Belcher promised the Grand Council members in the "french territories" that accession to the compact would place their people on the "wide and fruitful Field of English liberties."

Belcher explained to the assembled leaders from all the seven districts of the Mi'kmaq Nation that their burying of the Hatchets was a "sign of putting [them] in full possession of English Protection and Liberty." The "Field of English liberties," Chief Justice Belcher assured them, would be "free from the baneful weeds of Fraud and Subtlety." "The Laws," he continued, clearly stated the Crown's intent to create legally binding rights and "will be like a great Hedge about your Rights and properties — if any break this Hedge and hurt or injure you, the heavy weight of the Law will fall upon them and furnish their disobedience" (CO 217/18/276; PANS MSS Doc. Vol. 27, No. 14:699-700).

The Mi'kmaq reliance on the rule of law to resolve disputes with the immigrants demonstrates the separate and distinct jurisdictions between the Natives and immigrants. It demonstrates Mi'kmaq refusal to be placed under local political authorities or under criminal law. Instead, the Compact established the Civil Law of England — the fundamental principles of contract, property, and torts — as the appropriate legal and social standards of conduct between the Mi'kmaq and British in Nova Scotia (in Boldt, Long and Little Bear, 1985: 185-220).

The separate and distinct jurisdiction of tribal government from British settlements was firmly established in British law in America since 1749 (Mohegan Indians v. Connecticut. Record Book of Proceeding 1743:118). In the Royal Proclamation of 1763, His Majesty reserved the separate jurisdiction to the Mi'kmaq Nation in Atlantic Canada as their reserved Hunting Grounds (Slattery, in Boldt, Long and Little Bear, 1985: 114-147). The exclusive role delegated to Nova Scotia by the Crown was protecting Mi'kmaq treaty rights. After the 1761 accession Treaties, in 1762, the Assembly enacted an Act to Prevent Fraudulent Dealings in the Trade with the Indians (S.N.S. 1762, c. 3) which incorporated the Crown's promises of protections under the civil law. The Act created the procedure to implement Article 8 of the Prerogative Compact directly into Nova Scotia law. The Act stated that because the "Indians" are "unacquainted with the law of this province and in what manner they are to proceed in order to do themselves right," the Lieutenant Governor, Council, and Legislative Assembly authorized,

> the Governor, Lieutenant Governor, or Commander in Chief, upon complaint of any Indians within this province made to him or either of them, that they have been wronged or cheated of their furs or any other merchandise, or in any other their trade and dealing with other His Majesty Subjects; that the Governor, Lieutenant-Governor, or Commander in Chief, is hereby desired to direct His Majesty's Attorney General to prosecute the same, either before His Majesty's Justices, or in any of His Majesty's Courts of Record in a summary way, as the laws do direct, and such prosecution shall be deemed legal, and the judgement and execution shall issue accordingly.

There was no suggestion in the 1762 Act that the same obligations of other British subjects or coercive penalties by the Crown were to be extended to either Mi'kmaq Hunting Grounds or Mi'kmaq personally. Disputes among the Mi'kmaq were resolved under the customary *habenquedouic* law of the Nation.

The Crown's jurisdiction over the British settlers and immigrants to Nova Scotia, who were the third party beneficiaries of the Compact, was different from jurisdiction over the Mi'kmaq. Article 8 establishes a clear criterion for His Majesty's courts to judge the conduct of the British settlers with the Mi'kmaq. British civil law clearly defined a universal code to resolve the conflicts inherent in society to maintain collective or individual rights and advantages of the Mi'kmaq against involuntary losses. It gave the emigres' fair warning of the conduct that the Crown expected of them in relations to the Mi'kmaq. The Compact applied the civil law standards to the immigrants interacting with the Mi'kmaq. The operation of both His Majesty's civil and criminal law provided sufficient legal protection and remedies for any abuse of the Compact or of the Mi'kmaq by the British settlers.

The Mi'kmaq and the Crown

The Crown never placed the Mi'kmaq, personally or territorially, under provincial or federal criminal jurisdiction. This fact was first recognized in 1823 by Nova Scotia Judge T.C. Haliburton. Judge Haliburton noted that, while the Mi'kmaq are considered British subjects under their Treaty in respect of their right in royal courts, "yet they never litigate or in any way are impleaded. They have a code of traditional and customary law among themselves" (Nova Scotia 1823:65). The customary tribal law, called *habenquedouic* among the Mi'kmaq, still exists within the Aboriginal powers of the Grand Council of Mi'kmaq Nation. These fundamental principles were so firmly entrenched in the Mi'kmaq mind that no formal document outlining them was ever considered necessary.

The habenquedouic law of the Mi'kmaq is based on a tort principle of criminal law. It embodies the principle that he or she did not begin the offence; he or she has paid the aggrieved part back, and everyone quits and becomes good friends. The guilty one, even in killings, can repent his or her fault and makes satisfaction by offering presents and other suitable atonements to the aggrieved party. The idea of crimes against the sovereign or society was unknown to the Mi'kmaq law.

Judge Haliburton's observations of Mi'kmaq customary law are consistent with Crown precedents of other Native protectorates in the United Kingdom. The British courts have held that Aboriginal *lex loci* of Native protectorates continues to be valid law and is sufficient to plead immunity from ordinary legal process, except where otherwise provided by the prerogative Treaties (in Boldt, Long and Little Bear, 1985: 195-207).

As Mi'kmaq came into increasing conflict with the immigrants who encroached on their reserved hunting grounds, however, the local criminal justice system was not sufficient to overcome the racism and applied self interests of the new European settlers. The local courts and juries often became the deadliest enemies of the Mi'kmaq treaty and statutory rights.

Consistent with Article 8 of the Compact and the prerogative Acts, between 1842-1867, nevertheless, the Nova Scotia Assembly enacted the Indian Act and Indian Reserve Act to protect lands reserved for the Mi'kmaq from intrusion or unauthorized settlements. These acts modified the 1762 Act procedure. They authorized the Commissioner of Indian Affairs, rather than the Attorney General, to "proceed by information in the name of Her Majesty before Her Majesty's Supreme Court at Halifax or in the county where the Lands may lie, notwithstanding the legal title by Grant or otherwise, may not be vested in Her Majesty" (S.N.S. 1842: section V).

Notwithstanding these Acts, the criminal justice system failed the Crown and the Mi'kmaq. By 1849, it was obvious that Her Majesty's courts in Nova Scotia refused to enforce either the Compact, the prerogative Instructions, or the Indian Act. The Indian Commissioner reported to the Legislative Assembly that,

> Under present circumstances, no adequate protection can be obtained for Indian property. It would be vain to seek a verdict from any jury in this Island against the trespassers on the Reserves; nor perhaps would a member of the Bar be found willingly and effectually to advocate the cause of the Indians, inasmuch as he would thereby injure his own prospect, by damaging his popularity (LANSJ 1849: 356).

This is the initial version of the legal consciousness, "don't put your balls in a vice over an Indian."

In spite of the failure of the local justice systems, the British Crown, independently or in Imperial Parliament, never ratified the injustice. No subsequent prerogative Instruction or Acts of Parliament has ever expressly extended criminal jurisdiction over Mi'kmaq personally or over their reserved lands in derogation of their prerogative Treaty or the 1763 Proclamation (Foreign Jurisdiction Act (U.K.) 6 & & Vict. c. 94 (1843); Colonial Law Validity Act (U.K.) 1865).

Moreover, as a matter of British law, the Crown could not convey greater authority to the province or the federal government in 1867 than the Grand Council had originally conveyed to the Crown in the Compact. The Crown's authority was not inherent over the Mi'kmaq Nation in

North America; it was delegated by express terms of the Treaty. Neither the immigrants nor their elected politicians had authority to violate the prerogative order.

Under Sections 91(24) and 132 of the Constitution Act, 1867 and Section 35 of the Constitution Act, 1982 the treaty rights of the Mi'kmaq Nation have remained a constitutionally protected tribal jurisdiction. Under Section 52 (1) of the 1982 Act, Aboriginal and treaty rights are part of the Supreme Law of Canada; any law that is inconsistent with the provisions of the Constitution is, to the extent of the inconsistency, of no force or effect. Thus, it is arguable, as the Grand Council asserted, that the application of the Criminal Code to Mi'kmaq is unconstitutional and illegitimate.

The Mi'kmaq argument is that they have never consented to the federal parliament's application of criminal rules to Mi'kmaq. They have a treaty relationship directly with the sovereign of the United Kingdom, not with either the regimes of Atlantic Canada or the federal government. They have never agreed to the original compact creating the federal government in 1867; thus its administrative transfer of all matters relating to *Indians* and lands reserved to them, neither affected the status of the Mi'kmaq Nation in the United Kingdom nor granted criminal jurisdiction over Mi'kmaq or their reserved lands to the federal parliament. The federal authority to enact criminal law was limited to the immigrants' provinces and others who expressly joined the Confederation. The Grand Council has never expressly joined the Confederation and has been historically denied direct representation in the federal parliament and a vote in its selection.

In other parts of Canada, beginning with Treaty 2, the signatory tribes agreed to criminal jurisdiction off the reserved lands of Canada. They promised that they "will, in all respects, obey and abide by the law" and will aid in prosecuting offences against local law in the country ceded. Most of the numbered treaties specifically authorize the enforcement of federal "Indian" liquor laws on reserved lands. The "obey and abide" jurisdictional clauses demonstrate that neither the federal laws nor provincial administration of justice applied to reserves without their express consent. Thus, other treaties resolve the issues of criminal jurisdiction over *Indians* and their reserved lands in Canada, rather than federal statutes and provincial courts which implemented the treaty rights.

The Mi'kmaq have no similar legal or social compact with the federal government. Parliament cannot show any traditional, historical, or bureaucratic authority over the Grand Council of the Mi'kmaq Nation. Although attached administratively to the federal government by the Crown, neither the Grand Council nor the Mi'kmaq have ever accepted that the federal parliament ought, or has the right, to make decisions or law inconsistent with their Aboriginal and treaty rights.

In the absence of a clear "obey and abide" delegation to the Crown in right of Canada, the Grand Council has retained its ancient jurisdiction over all persons and subjects within their reserved hunting grounds, that is, those lands which were never ceded to or purchased by the Crown, under the 1763 Royal Proclamation. Because no part of the national territory was ever ceded to the Crown by subsequent agreements with the Governor of Nova Scotia or Canada, the Grand Council maintained its territorial jurisdiction, in theory and fact, over Mi'kmaq in their hunting grounds. Similarly, the province has retained jurisdiction over the immigrants.

Conclusions

Throughout the Marshall Inquiry, the Attorney General of Nova Scotia maintained that, in the administration of justice, the *Indians* have a formal equality with other citizens. This assimilationist philosophy is unique to the criminal justice system. It is not present in the delivery of any other fundamental services to Mi'kmaq in the province (for example, health, welfare, and education). The federal government still contracts with Nova Scotia to provide essential services to Mi'kmaq in such areas; thus creating a fiscal interest in the province for continued funding. The criminal justice system is the only service which the province applies to *Indians*, without charging the federal government.

While at first glance the assimilationist attitude would seem to fit within traditional notions of equality and fair play, and most Canadians would no doubt perceive this attitude as pro-*Indian*, the Grand Council has most often taken quite a different view. The assimilationist philosophy contains many elements, some of which have a surface attraction, such as allowing the Mi'kmaq to share in the educational, material, et cetera, benefits of provincial society. There are, however, several basic flaws to this view. The provincial attitude of formal equality of *Indians* is seen by the Grand Council as another attempt to destroy Aboriginal tribal institutions and, in effect, deprives the Mi'kmaq people of their Aboriginal and treaty rights, and forces them to assimilate individually into provincial society.

The fact that theories of social darwinism and assimilation would have more force over administration of justice in Canada than the existing treaty rights illustrates the operation of a contradiction and ambiguity of constitutional phrases of a federal government "similar in principle to that of the United Kingdom" and its emergency powers of "Peace, Order and good Government" in the Constitution Act, 1867. In the absence of clear political principles in the constitutional document, successive political parties and governments expounded and implemented differing interpretations of the underlying basis of Canadian legal and political life. There were no clear limitations to interfere with their policy.

This implicit assimilationist philosophy towards individual Mi'kmaw in provincial society has always been opposed by the Mi'kmaq, and is now repudiated by the federal government. What the Mi'kmaq Nation desires is a political integration into Canadian federalism on a basis of equality. Individual integration has failed. It must be noted that the assumption of criminal jurisdiction over *Indians* since 1940 has not resulted in the integration of Mi'kmaq into the dominant culture; nor has it provided substantial nondiscriminatory services to the Mi'kmaq. On the contrary, as the Marshall Inquiry illustrated, it has alienated the Mi'kmaq and imprisoned them in federal jails.

A Mi'kmaw has three possible responses to the knowledge that most Nova Scotians categorize him or her as inferior. Each response has its characteristic political expression. A Mi'kmaw may adopt the view of himself which the majority has of him; he may believe in his own inferiority and hence the "culture of poverty." Or the Mi'kmaw may deny the relevance of the category of race altogether, argue for equality and press for integration and attempt to will away the racism. Or the Mi'kmaw can acknowledge the identity given to him or her by the majority, but not accept the evaluation, and search for methods of maintaining his or her own values with dignity.

The Grand Council has always chosen the latter method. It is seen as the only authentic choice which affirms and maintains fidelity with our ancestors' legal and political legacy and cultural integrity. The Mi'kmaq have very little faith in attempting to change the attitude and norms of the dominant society. Because the moral conceptions of what an *Indian* is are rooted in mores, which change slowly, the Grand Council does not think it practical to will away the brown colours from the image of the "wild savage" that haunts the minds of Canadians. This image provided much of the Canadian policy behind infantilization of the *Indians* and forced them into total dependence on the dominant social groups.

More importantly, the assimilationist philosophy of the provincial government ignores the new constitutional era of Canadian federalism. It ignores that even the generality of the Constitution Acts of Canada and the Charter of Rights is limited by existing Aboriginal and treaty rights. It continues to wrongfully assume that tribal institutions are transitional to provincial authority, rather than their declared future role as primary structures of future program delivery to Mi'kmaq. The philosophy assumes that Aboriginal and treaty rights are not collective rights but, rather, apply to individual *Indians* because of their race. Most of the provincial arguments, therefore, are cast in terms of extending full citizenship to individuals of a race, with little or no reference to the tribal relationship with the Crown or the meaning of membership in a protected tribal culture.

In an interesting twist of logic and historical reality, the province also defines Mi'kmaq tribal identity as separatism, and, hence, unconstitutional segregation. Faced with systemic racism in the province, it is baseline racism to assume that, because the cultural rights, traditions, and institutions of the Mi'kmaq are different from those of the dominant society, they are legally or culturally inferior.

The absence of an understanding of the unique status of Mi'kmaq political culture in the constitutional order of Canada, allowed the legal consciousness to disregard the separate and distinct prerogative jurisdiction of the Mi'kmaq Nation. More than establishing the civil court as the protector of Mi'kmaq rights, the Crown promised the Mi'kmaq that when they applied to the civil courts they would have equal protection of the law. Thus, more than two hundred years before the Charter of Rights was placed in the Canadian constitution, the Mi'kmaq were given equal right to life, liberty, and security of their persons and property by the civil law. Although the Mi'kmaq were under a different jurisdiction from that of the settlers, before the courts they were to have the "same benefits, advantages and privileges as others of His Majesty Subjects." This section of the Compact is amenable to the interpretation that a Mi'kmaw is protected from both substantive and procedural unfair impositions from the Crown.

The equivalent wording of section 15(1) of the Canadian Charter states that,

> Every individual is equal before and under the law and has the right to the equal protection and equal benefit of the law without discrimination and, in particular, without discrimination based on race, national, or ethnic order, colour, religion, sex, age or mental or physical disability

Distinct from the Charter, however, the Compact guarantees are not subject to any reasonable limits prescribed by provincial law as can be demonstrably justified in a free and democratic society.

The federal criminal codes are valid for the immigrants because they create an artificial order necessary for interest group pluralism in Canada. But an artificial order is not general or autonomous when applied to Mi'kmaq. When such an order is imposed over vested treaty rights and acts that respect the natural order of the Mi'kmaq Nation and are part of the supreme law of Canada, the validity of the legislation is questionable. It is seen as a system or preserve existing in inequalities between the immigrants and the Aboriginal peoples created by the era of social darwinism.

The supposed reconciliation of values by the federal parliament could be of no force and effect. It is viewed as a weapon of personal and cultural oppression. The fact is that the legitimacy of the criminal law by parliament is justified by the immigrants' conception of social order and the doctrine of private interests and is not a neutral doctrine. While it may adequately describe Western European society, such interest group pluralism is seen as an oppressive and alien theory to Mi'kmaq society.

To achieve equality before and under the law and the right to the equal protection and equal benefit of the law, the Grand Council emphasised to the Commission that Mi'kmaq require substantive equality rather than formal equality. Mi'kmaq have to be treated as people who have immunities from the general law because of their ancestors' agreement with the Crown. Tribal courts will have to handle local disputes between Mi'kmaq, and to review extradition of Mi'kmaq before a change of venue to federal courts. Some of these procedures already exist in the Criminal Code, but the formal equality of the law hides their application to the Mi'kmaq and, thus, to members of the Mi'kmaq Nation, such as Donald Marshall, Jr.

Notes

[1] For clarity, the use of "Inquiry" shall refer to all the attorneys, witnesses and reporters who participated on a daily basis before the Commission. The term "Commission" refers to the three judges and its staff.

Table of Cases

Advocate-General of Bengal v. Ranee Suree Surnomoye (1863)
A.G. of Nova Scotia v. A.G. Canada [1951] S.C.R. 31
Freeman v. Fairlie (1828) 1 Moo. P.C. 305)
Guerin v. Queen [1985] 2 S.C.R. 376
Mohegan Indian v. Connecticut Colony (1773) Record Book of Proceedings
    Jan. 15 (P.C.)
Matz v Arnett, (1973) 412 U.S. 481
Patriation Reference ,(1981) 125 D.L.R. (3d) 1)
R. v. Isaac (1975) 13 N.S.R. (2d) 460 (N.S.S.C.A.D.)
    January 1, 1980
Seymour v. Superintendent, (1962) 368 U.S. 351
Simon v. Queen [1985] S.C.R 239; (1982) 49 N.S.R. (2d) 566)
Worcester v. Georgia, (1832) 31 U.S. (6 Pet.) 515

Statutes

Act to prevent Fraudulent Dealings in the Trade with the Indians (S.N.S. 1762, c. 3)
An Act concerning Indian Reserves S.N.S. 1859, c. 44 30 May 1859.
Constitution Act, 1867
Constitution Act, 1982 Canada Gazette (part 1) vol. 116, no. 17 at 2927-8.
Elekewaki Compact, 1752, 26 Geo. II.
Foreign Enlistment Act, 33 & 34 Vict. c. 90
Foreign Jurisdiction Act, 6 & 7 Vict. c. 94, 1890 (UK 53 & 54 Vict. c. 37)
Indian Act, S.N.S. 1842, c. 16
Indian Act, 1867
Nova Scotia Proclamation of 4 May 1762, 3 Geo III
Royal Proclamation of 1763, 4 Geo. III, British Public Record Office:c. 66/3693.

References

Akins, Charles, ed.*Selections from the Public Documents of Nova Scotia*. Halifax: Charles Annand, 1869.

Black, Edwin R. *Divided Loyalties. Canadian Concepts of Federalism*. McGill-Queen's University Press, 1975.

Boldt, Menno and J.A. Long, eds. *The Quest for Justice: Aboroginal Peoples and Aboriginal Rights*. University of Toronto Press, 1985.

Chitty, Joseph. *A Treatus on the Law of the Prerogatives of the Crown*. London: Joseph Butterworth and Son, 1830

CO: Correspondence between the Governor and the Colonial Office, Public Record Office London.

DIAND: (Department of Indian Affairs and Northern Development). *Statement of the Government of Canada on Indian Policy*. [White Paper]. Queen's Printer, 1969

Haliburton, T. C. *Nova Scotia*. 1823

Hawthorn, H.B. *A Survey of the Contemporary Indians of Canada: Economic, Political, Educational Needs and Policies*, 2 vols. Ottawa: Queen's Printer, 1966-67

LJNS: Journal Legislative Assemby Nova Scotia.

Lindly, M.F. *The Acquistion and Government of Backward Territory in International Law.* London: Longmans, Green and Co., 1926

Indian Self-Government, Report of the Special Committee on Indian Self-Government to the House of Commons. Ottawa: Queen's Printer [Penner Report], 1983.

Murdock, Beamish *Epitome of the Laws of Nova Scotia* 1832.

PAC: Public Archives of Canada.

PANS: Public Archives of Nova Scotia. MSS Doc. Vol. 27, No. 14:699-700).

Patterson, Lisa Lynne. "Indian Affairs and the Nova Scotia Centralization Policy" (unpublished M.A. (History) thesis. Dalhousie University, 1985

Report, The Select Committte on Aborigines of the British Settlements 26 June 1837, Command Papers (UK).

Weaver, Sally M. *Making Canadian Indian Policy.* University of Toronto Press, 1981.

The Social Construction of Ethnic Containment: The Royal Commission on the Donald Marshall Jr. Prosecution

Joy A. Mannette

The Marshall Case

On the night of May 28 1971, in Sydney[1], Nova Scotia's Wentworth Park, a sixteen year old Black man was stabbed in the abdomen. He died the next evening in Sydney City Hospital. The following Friday, a Mi'kmaq[2] man was charged with second degree murder. In November 1971, seventeen-year-old Donald "Junior" Marshall, eldest son of the Grand Chief of the Mi'kmaq Nation[3], was found guilty of the murder of the Black man, Sanford "Sandy" William Seale. Marshall was Membertou *Indian*; Seale was Whitney Pier *Black*.[4] Thus began the Marshall Case.

Sentenced to life imprisonment, Junior Marshall served eleven years in federal institutions at Dorchester, New Brunswick, and Springhill, Nova Scotia. Throughout the incarceration, Marshall protested his innocence, periodically checking leads with the help of those on the outside.[5] These efforts finally spurred a new RCMP investigation. On May 10, 1983, Donald Marshall, Jr. was acquitted by the Nova Scotia Supreme Court of the murder of Sandy Seale. Though legally free, the judicial process indicted Marshall as the author of his own misery, while exonerating itself:

> ... any miscarriage of justice is, however, more apparent than real.... There can be no doubt that Donald Marshall's untruthfulness through this whole affair contributed in large measure to his conviction. (Appeal Division of the Nova Scotia Supreme Court Judgement, May 10, 1983.)

The Marshall Inquiry

Pressure to call an inquiry into the Donald Marshall Case mounted; much of this was orchestrated by the media.[6] On May 13, 1987, the province of Nova Scotia convened a Royal Commission[7]

> with power to inquire into, report . . . findings, and make recommendations to the Governor in Council respecting the investigation of the death of Sanford William Seale on the 28th-29th day of May, A.D., 1971; the charging and prosecution of Donald Marshall, Jr. with that death; the subsequent conviction and sentencing of Donald Marshall, Jr., for the non-capital murder of Sanford William Seale for which he was subsequently found to be not guilty; and such related matters which the Commissioners consider relevant to the Inquiry(Nova Scotia Order in Council, October 28, 1986).

On September 9, 1987, the Royal Commission on the Donald Marshall, Jr. Prosecution began public hearings in St. Andrews Church Hall in downtown Sydney, Nova Scotia. The venue of public hearings concluded in Halifax, Nova Scotia in June 1988.

On January 26, 1990, the Royal Commission on the Donald Marshall, Jr. Prosecution released its seven-volume report. The Marshall Inquiry had granted full standing to fifteen parties, ranging from individual actors to collective interests, and observer status to two. The Inquiry had held ninety-three days of public hearings; collected 16,390 pages of transcript evidence given by 113 witnesses; examined 176 exhibits entered in evidence during the hearings; held two-and-one-half days of expert presentations; and solicited five volumes of research by leading scholars. The total cost to the public purse was eight million dollars. In a stinging indictment of jurisprudence, the Commissioners' Report concluded:

> The criminal justice system failed Donald Marshall, Jr. at virtually every turn from his arrest and wrongful conviction for murder in 1971 up to, and even beyond, his acquittal by the Court of Appeal in 1983. The tragedy of the failure is compounded by evidence that this miscarriage of justice could — and should — have been prevented, or at least corrected quickly, if those involved in the system had carried out their duties in a professional and/or competent manner. That they did not is due, in part at least, to the fact that Donald Marshall, Jr. is a Native. (Digest of Findings, 1989:1).

Thus, from within a quasi-judicial framework and coached in juridical discourse, the Marshall Inquiry argued that "what went wrong" was a malfunction of an essentially reformable system. The integrity of the judicial *system* was not impugned. On the contrary, it was human fallibility, in the guise of individual incompetence, which caused the apparent systemic breakdown. Secondly, through its own actions and consistent with due process, the Marshall Inquiry was able to demonstrate, publicly, through its instruction and educative functions, that the desired juridical epistemology and bureaucratic practices, which had been called into question, *can* ensure that justice is done. In this sense, the combination of targeting human fallibility and instructing by example resulted in the Marshall Inquiry's ability to allay public doubt about judicial process, state legal coherence, and administrative rationality.

Finally, the Marshall Inquiry confronted the shattered societal consensus about the law which had disintegrated in the face of allegations which were representatively brought before the Inquiry (for example, of juridical failure, of racism). Through the insertion of minority representatives into the Inquiry process (for example, Marshall's lawyers and lawyers representing Oscar Seale, father of Sandy Seale, the Union of Nova Scotia Indians, and the Black United Front of Nova Scotia), the Marshall Inquiry was able to re-establish a discourse of unity and cohesion among Inquiry representatives, which was expressed by minority adherence to, and endorsement of, the Inquiry Report.

The Marshall Inquiry was indeed an "opportunity to put the state on trial"; however, it was a "trial in which no one goes to jail" (Salter, 1988:2). However, the fractured hegemony called into question by the Marshall Case is also an *ethnic* hegemony and the hegemonic order which the Marshall Inquiry sought to restore is also an ethnic one. Yet, as Grand Captain Alex Denny of the Mi'kmaq Nation commented on the inquiry process, "you can't be the doctor, if you are the disease" (in henderson, 1989:11).

Ethnic Hegemony

According to Brand and Bhaggiyadatta (1986:7), to understand the nature of Canadian racism, it is necessary to address the "culture of everyday." By culture, they mean the common aspects of everyday life which are usually not seen as controversial. Rather, their commonplace nature renders them unproblematic. Historically-constituted and historically-specific, the culture of everyday is continually and "incrementally" constructed. Bearing the whole range of social relations (for example, law, economy, gender, etc.), the culture of everyday is expressed in the ways we speak, words we use, looks, gestures, silences, and physical movements. Brand and Bhaggiyadatta (1986:7) argue that the culture of racism, as a component of the culture of everyday, is comprised of both apparently random and institutionalized ways in which racism conditions commonplace activities. It is postulated here that one institutional expression of racism is carried by the quasi-judicial format of commissions of inquiry.

Critical assessments of Canadian multicultural practice and theory have compellingly documented the social constructions of "other" which animate these liberal applications (Moore, 1980; Peter, 1981; Young, ed., 1987). This is particularly obvious in the notion of a unified and non-ethnic "Canadian society" to which "others" may contribute normatively. So embedded in Canadian society is racism that its operation is taken-for-granted, a key component of how things work.

Snider (1988) has suggested that nowhere is the taken-for-granted character of social life so apparent as with the law. Indeed, following Marchak (1988), we may identify the ideological terrain of jurisprudence as particularly impervious to reflective scrutiny. As Snider (1988:31) has pointed out:

> Law has been reified into a quasimystical, quasireligious entity whose formation is above the competitive struggle for supremacy that goes on in ... every ... institution we know of.

Significantly, commissions of inquiry provide a quasi-judicial format for the assignment of blame and the delineation of cause. In other words, the commission of inquiry operates according to the same suspect logic and practices which caused the crisis in institutional confidence in the first place.

henderson (1989) has argued that the Marshall Inquiry was forced to examine the question of systemic racism through the application of juridical conventions. Calling for a wider understanding of ethnocentrism, Wall (1988:10) has focused on the group myopia of juridical actors. As such, he has postulated that the over-investment of juridical actors in the integrity of the justice system "was one of the reasons why Donald Marshall, Jr. was convicted and spent eleven years in jail." I concur with henderson (1989) that the Marshall Inquiry could not explore systemic racism, given its biological, as opposed to cultural, understanding of race.[8] For example, the Marshall Inquiry persisted in identifying Junior Marshall as *Indian*, a generic category which is apparently visible and may be scientifically ascertained (that is, rooted in physiology and genetics).

I also agree with Wall's (1988) position that the structural relevances of juridical process render it an unlikely paradigm within which to critique itself.[9] However, the Inquiry's attempts to explore connections between racial attitudes and racist actions provide us with important documentation of the very culture of everyday which animates racial "maps of meaning" (Hall et al., 1981:54), underscores racism in practice (Brand and Bhaggiyadatta, 1986), and socially produces "others" in Canadian society (Young, 1987). Marshall Inquiry testimony resonates with the interpretive frameworks, modes of speech, looks, gestures, and silences which are commonplace expressions of institutionalized, or systemic, racism (Mannette, 1990). For example, Marshall Inquiry testimony delineates police associations of *Indians* with crime; references Mi'kmaq people as "Indians," "wagon-burners," "broken arrows"; and denies connections between Mi'kmaq social segregation on reserves and the absence of the Membertou Reserve from maps of the city of Sydney. This litany of apartness is the grammar and punctuation of marginal existence.[10]

Tribal Culture and the Marshall Inquiry

Marshall Inquiry testimony also articulates the existence and dimensions of a tribal culture, whose worldview, though dominantly maligned, organizes Mi'kmaq social life. Eleanor Johnson (1991:7) has described the essence of Mi'kmaq tribal culture:

> Esteem for elders, sharing and cooperation, respect for man and nature are the inherent qualities of tribal consciousness still prevalent in the Mi'kmaq Nation. That is the culture of the People, the spirit of their dignity as humans. Tribal consciousness provides an alternative perspective in a dominant non-native culture. The Mi'kmaq Nation endures and thrives as a result of the values that they adhere to in this modern capitalist society. It is not the accumulation of objects, "nouns" in an English word, but one's service to others that distinguishes Mi'kmaq from others. It is a mentality that has to be addressed, to understand Mi'kmaq history and European mythology....

Tribal culture enters into the official discourse of the Marshall Inquiry. In order to discharge due process and instruct through example, a commission of inquiry must give voice to all parties. The interesting question, of course, is what weight the inquiry process assigns to minority testimony in its final report, where it assigns blame, defines the problem, and delineates solutions. Elsewhere, I argued that minority interpretations were not part of the "preferred reading" of events chronicled by the Marshall Commission (Mannette, 1988). However, for our purposes here, it is sufficient to point to the tribal voice from the margins which has been publicly amplified through the Marshall Inquiry process. That tribal voice from the margins did not fracture the ethnic hegemony which the Marshall Inquiry sought to restore. It does, however, signal structures of hegemonic resistance which provide "minor liberations" (Willis, 1981) for Mi'kmaq People.

A crucial way in which the Mi'kmaq interpretive framework manifested itself in testimony before the Marshall Inquiry involves what happens when Mi'kmaq people encounter the judicial process. Bruce Wildsmith (1988: 18), lawyer representing the Union of Nova Scotia Indians before the Inquiry, summarized testimony of Sydney psychiatrist, Dr. Mian:

> Indians respond to anxiety provoking situations, such as testifying in court, giving evidence in their own defence, or giving statements to police, by becoming quieter and quieter. They tend to withdraw, be aloof and detached.

How this was manifested in Mi'kmaq behaviour in the judicial process may be examined. For example, the transcript of Marshall's original trial (R. v. Donald Marshall, Jr.[1971], Vol.II: 186-93) carries frequent admonitions from lawyers and judge to seventeen-year-old Marshall to "speak up" (II/187/31), to "put that hand down Donnie" (II/188/17) and generally to answer questions more fully. It is interesting to note the understanding of Marshall's Inquiry Counsel, Anne Derrick, Marlys Edwardh and Clayton Ruby, on this point. Marshall's Counsel constructed his reluctance to be photographed and grilled when giving testimony only in psychological terms (for example, anxiety, fear). Despite the fact that he gave testimony in Mi'kmaq, facilitated by an interpreter, Marshall's cultural unease with the process was not understood and not raised by his Counsel as a crucial factor in encounters between Mi'kmaq people and the non-Native judicial process.

In his submission before the Inquiry, Union of Nova Scotia Indians' lawyer, Bruce Wildsmith, illustrated this point with reference to another Mi'kmaq witness, Artie Paul:

> The emotional and psychological difficulties many Indians face in coming to court were effectively illustrated before this Commission by Arthur J. Paul. The first time he was scheduled to give evidence he came to the hall in the morning, "felt pretty tense," had a pain in the chest, felt he was getting sick and left (Paul 24/4360-61). Then on the day he did begin his testimony, he became

confused and the Commission adjourned early (23/4325) (Paul, cited in Wildsmith, 1988:22).

Crucially, however, from the point of arguing for culturally sensitive judicial processes, psychologizing "institutional bars and bureaucratic impediments" (Dahlie and Fernando, 1981: 1) does little to further the erosion of institutional ethnocentrism.

It is interesting, as well, to note how unwieldy the Inquiry found Marshall's testimony given in Mi'kmaq through interpreter Noel Knockwood. This was in spite of previous Inquiry testimony which called for interpreters when Mi'kmaq people gave testimony. As Mi'kmaq linguist Bernie Francis had indicated:

> Jr. Marshall's English was... very poor in a formal setting. I think that there would be an awful lot that he wouldn't understand (22/3930).

Bernie Francis concurred that, "in most cases Native people needed interpreters and in most cases they weren't granted interpreters" (22/3935) Bernie Francis identified juridical conventions as the stumbling block since "[prosecutors] found the art of cross-examination to be very difficult when they were doing it through an interpreter" (22/3935).

Mi'kmaq unfamiliarity and unease with judicial process were noted frequently in testimony before the Marshall Inquiry. 1971 Marshall lawyer Simon Khattar assessed Marshall as a "terrible witness, bad witness, poor witness" (25/4757). RCMP Sergeant Carroll identified Marshall as a "typical Indian witness... in that he spoke in a low voice and he was not volunteering much" (49/9110-11). Carroll labelled such behaviour in *Indian* witnesses as "passive" (49/9111). Cape Breton Hospital psychiatrist, Dr. Mian, suggested that white juridical actors might not understand that such behaviour was culturally specific and that its meaning in white culture and in Mi'kmaq culture was not the same. In addition, it is important to note that the Mi'kmaq language does not have words for "please" and "excuse me," or even one to signal the end of conversation. Thus, western concepts of politeness do not orient Mi'kmaq thought and action. However, the absence of these does not signal disrespect. As Bernie Francis summed it up:

> A Native person (would) walk into a courtroom with his hat sort of under his arm, hair a little bit messy, perhaps lumberjack boots, lumberjack sweater; just want to get out of there so fast, that they would do anything or say anything to do just that. And

> they felt extremely uncomfortable in the courtroom and they felt very lowly and they didn't really know what to expect. All they wanted was to ... get out of there no matter what (22/3941).

Mi'kmaq cultural unease with involvement in judicial process appears to be complemented by disrespect from white actors. Former Mi'kmaq court worker, Eva Gould, gave evidence before the Inquiry, in reference to the attitude of the crown prosecutor:

> ...there was not as much courtesy, not as much respect, and it was as if, "Get this over with and get you out of my way. You're a nuisance and a bother, the whole works of you" (73/13015).

Further, whites in the judicial process, empathetic to the situation of Native people, could be "warned off" by colleagues, as in the case of Felix Cacchione [then Marshall's lawyer, now a Nova Scotia provincial family court judge]. Cacchione was advised by Judge Robert Anderson, former Director-Criminal in the Nova Scotia Attorney-General's Department, "Felix, don't get your balls caught in a vice over an Indian." And, as RCMP Staff Sergeant Wheaton reported before the Inquiry, at the 1987 annual RCMP regimental dinner, then Nova Scotia Attorney General Ron Giffin delivered "approximately five to ten minutes of slapstick comedy in reference to the Marshall case" (43/7938). Disrespect for Mi'kmaq people is also illustrated by the lack of Membertou input in RCMP investigations:

> RCMP Inspector Alan Marshall, in carrying out his review in 1971 of Jimmy MacNeil's story that Roy Ebsary was the real killer, admitted that useful and reliable information could have been had from the Indian community at Membertou, yet he contacted no one and instead relied exclusively on sources connected to police in one way or another. (Wildsmith, 1988:40)

Within the judicial process, a particularly significant way in which Mi'kmaq and white worldviews collide is in terms of the conception of guilt. As Bernie Francis testified, "Micmacs misunderstood the word "guilty" because there is no such word in the Micmac language" (22/3935). Ruth Holmes Whitehead (1988:15) has elaborated on this point:

> One of the hardest concepts for Europeans to deal with was the belief held by the People that there was no individual guilt. There was only tribal (or band, or family) guilt, and therefore revenge could be taken on the "innocent" members of the guilty

individual's group, just as acceptably as on the actual offender. When the part *is* the whole, then the whole is equally guilty with the part.[11]

Further, claims of innocence made by Mi'kmaq people would not have the resonance of white protestations within a juridical process organized around western worldviews. Bernie Francis explained:

> The Micmac language is very inflexional and expresses emphasis and emotions through words and endings rather than tone of voice. Thus a Micmac person expressed innocence without the raising of voice or becoming extremely emotional. . . . the misunderstanding might be that, "gee, this person is not very strong in his assertion about his innocence; therefore, there must be something there" (22/4082-84).

Judge Lewis Matheson of the Nova Scotia Supreme Court called such Mi'kmaq behaviour "reticent" (27/5038) before the Marshall Inquiry.

Official Discourse and Tribal Consciousness

Following Burton and Carlen (1979), the role of official discourse is to assign blame in terms of the temporary failure of an essentially reformable system. Emphasis on human fallibility is often made to reinforce the notion that, had actors adequately discharged their functions, the crisis which has led to state intervention would have been averted. Having been seen to publicly and authoritatively take charge in the assignment of blame, the state process of official discourse transforms an ideological phenomenon (that is, eroded public confidence in judicial process) into a material event (that is, the inquiry and its report). The material event is worked up according to principles of administrative rationality and legal coherence (for example, the use of lawyers, judges, quasi-judicial format, etc.). Of key importance is the representative inclusion of minority constituents. Through the inquiry process, via their lawyer representatives, minority factions are included and given voice. Crucially, some of their recommendations are incorporated into the majority findings. Thus, minority factions are seen to collude in the inquiry process and "consent" is manufactured.

The extent to which Mi'kmaq cultural expression violated western consensual norms still appears misunderstood by key juridical actors, ranging from Nova Scotia Supreme Court judges, who found Marshall culpable in his own conviction, to lawyers representing him before the Inquiry. While there is little understanding of the dimensions and significance of cultural differences on the part of juridical actors, analysis of Marshall Inquiry testimony does suggest the continued existence of an interpretive framework and modes of speech which are uniquely Mi'kmaq. The question of recognition and accommodation of this cultural difference by dominant institutions and their constituent players is part of what minority representatives (for example, the Union of Nova Scotia Indians) were attempting to achieve through the Inquiry process. This is particularly signalled by their call for a tribal justice system, which the province of Nova Scotia misunderstands as simply a matter of changing the race of the juridical actors.

What this brief overview suggests, however, is the distinct and non-western configuration of Mi'kmaq tribal society. It points to the plurality of culture consciousness and being which animates civil society — a diversity constantly subsumed by hegemonic initiatives. What the Marshall Inquiry offers us primarily is an exercise in ethnic containment to mend the fractured societal consensus occasioned by Junior Marshall's victimization as a Mi'kmaw. Mi'kmaq worldview emerges in the Marshall Inquiry, then, as an excluded, not preferred, interpretive framework within a dominant ethnic hegemonic order.

Notes

[1] Sydney, Nova Scotia, is a city of 35,000 in underdeveloped Atlantic Canada. Characterized by a declining coal and steel industry, the local economy has been in crisis since the 1930s and more seriously since the 1960s when the federal and provincial states stepped in to assume corporate responsibility for coal and steel production. There are disproportionately high rates of un- and underemployment. The majority of the working population (approximately 80 percent) is concentrated in the service sector which, in the 1990s, is increasingly in crisis, offers few benefits, and is characterized by low wages and part-time work.

The area projects an Anglo-Celtic culture which effectively camouflages the ethnic diversity (for example, Acadian, eastern European, Italian, Caribbean Black, etc.) initially attracted by the burgeoning industrialism in the first two decades of the twentieth century. Of crucial significance is that the heart and vitality of the local Native culture, Mi'kmaq, is concentrated on various reserves [Membertou, Eskasoni, Whycocomough, Wagmatcook, Chapel Island] within one hour's drive of the city. A split labour market (Bonacich, 1976) along ethnic lines has been maintained into the contemporary period. This includes the stereotypical welfarism associated with the reservation system and with the process of underdevelopment in Atlantic Canada.

[2] The Mi'kmaq, or "Allied Peoples," are one of the Algonquian tribes of the eastern woodlands of the Atlantic seaboard. Mi'kma'kik, or the traditional hunting grounds of the Mi'kmaq, ranged from present-day Newfoundland to

The Social Construction of Ethnic Containment

Massachusetts and west to the New Brunswick/Quebec border. Pre-contact, the Mi'kmaq Nation had a highly organized political and social system and were avid maritime venturers. The Mi'kmaq were peaceful and pragmatic hunters/gatherers who seasonally relocated to more advantageous sources of food supplies. Today, the Mi'kmaq in Nova Scotia are concentrated on thirteen mostly rural reserves, although there has been increased migration to the Halifax/Dartmouth urban area in the last ten years. The Mi'kmaq are one of the First Nations who have the longest experience with European contact. According to the Grand Council of the Mi'kmaq Nation,

> Freedom and liberty ... confrontation ... subjugation ... resistance — all of these words describe the current situation in Nova Scotia as it relates between Mi'kmaq people and our settler neighbours. Despite protections afforded by international and domestic law, a people are forcibly dispossessed of their land and resources, their governmental institutions are intentionally destabilized, their children are condemned to a bleak future based on poverty and dependency — all so that others can reap a profit. Some backwater Third World dictatorship? No, Canada (Nova Scotia). Such has been the history of the Mi'kmaq people. (Grand Council, 1989: 73-74).

[3] The Santé Mawi'omi Wijit Mi'kmaq, or the Grand Council of the Mi'kmaq Nation, is the traditional governance of the Mi'kmaq Nation. While decision-making on the Grand Council is not, and has never been, hierarchical, two key positions are the Kjisakamow [Grand Chief] and the Kjikeptin [Grand Captain]. Currently, in practice, the Kjisakamow is more a spiritual leader and the Kjikeptin is more a secular leader.

[4] Membertou Reservation is actually located within the boundaries of the city of Sydney but is spatially, culturally, and psychically separate from surrounding white neighbourhoods. If Membertou Reserve is one of Sydney's ethnic ghettos, Whitney Pier is the other. Since the turn of the century, when steel production drew in a labouring population, Whitney Pier has been an ethnic enclave. Concentrated here are Blacks, Italians, Ukrainians, Poles, Newfoundlanders, Acadian French, etc. Whitney Pier is separated from Sydney proper by the steel plant and there is only one connecting road, known as the "subway/overpass." To be from "the Pier" was, and continues to be, a pejorative designation.

[5] The two volumes of files of Roy Gould, Chief at Membertou in 1971 and past Director of the *Micmac News*, bear testimony to his efforts to win an appeal in Junior's case. These files include letters from politicians, state and other organizations, and concerned individuals. The most poignant letters are from Junior to Roy during the eleven years of incarceration.

[6] Following Marshall's 1983 acquittal, national, provincial, and local print media carried articles calling for an inquiry. A certain degree of political mileage was

made of the case by provincial opposition parties. Also, there was unease among some lawyers, some members of the provincial Bar Society, and some bureaucratic mandarins who saw the necessity to "clean house" and to do so publicly. Following Roy Ebsary's January 1985 conviction for manslaughter in the death of Sandy Seale, pressure on the province of Nova Scotia to call an inquiry became intense. Media activity tended to confirm the prevalent sense that a public inquiry was the appropriate vehicle for addressing the crisis which the Marshall Case had become.

7 Public inquiries are popular tactics in the state repertoire's response to hegemonic crisis (Burton and Carlen, 1979; Salter, 1988; Taylor, 1984). In Canada, since 1867, there have been "400 full-blown inquiries" (Sopinka, 1988). The public inquiry is useful to the state. The public nature of the inquiry ensures that the state is seen to be doing something, that is, exercising a leadership role in a crisis context. Further, as Hall et al. (1981) point out, the over-accessing of state representatives by media and media structural dependence on these authoritative voices, result in wide dissemination of inquiry activity. It is also the case that "Royal Commissions of Inquiry are set up to address an urgent public concern that is almost certainly politically sensitive" (Grenville, 1988:1).

8 My understanding of systemic racism has been informed by Bolaria and Li (1985:8):

> When we speak of institutional racism, we do not mean that a certain percentage of the population holds a negative view towards minority members, but, rather, racial ideologies are part of institutional practice, and race is a basis of stratification. To the extent that members of the dominant and subordinate groups have unequal access to rights and privileges, and that such inequality is institutionalized, and rationalized by a theory supporting the inherent superiority and inferiority of racial groups, then it is fair to say that race has become a basic feature of such a society.

henderson (1989:2) has pointed out the fundamental error of the Marshall Inquiry's definition of the Mi'kmaq in racial terms:

> The justice system has made race, instead of legal rights, the over-riding principle of organization. Race is the crucial symbol of the Mi'kmaq social role in Nova Scotian society. Colour of the skin became the criterion of a rigid set of expectations equating white with civilization and brown with savages.

henderson (1989:9-10) also has decried the practice of the Marshall Inquiry in accepting, unquestioningly, an understanding of race as biological fact.

[9] By structural relevances, Dorothy Smith (1974) referred to all of the structural components which came into play in the process of ideological construction of reality. Here she particularly flagged the significance of class, gender, and ethnicity.

[10] In *Marginal Notes*, Rick Salutin (1984) outlined the complex process of marginalization, the power of the "centre," and the roles which marginal people play in holding their marginalization in place, since they can never be a part of the centre.

[11] The stereotyping of all *Indians* as criminal on the basis of Marshall's apparent criminality seems a strange perversion of the tribal mandates of responsibility. Further, the anguish experienced by Marshall's family and community is additional evidence of a white-imposed punishment of the tribe.

References

Bolaria, B. Singh and Peter S. Li. *Racial Oppression in Canada*. Toronto: Garamond Press, 1985.

Bonacich, Edna. "Advanced Capitalism and Black/White Relations in the United States: A Split Labour Market Interpretation." *American Sociological Review*, 41 February: 34-51, 1976.

Brand, Dionne and Krisantha Sri Bhaggiyadatta. *Rivers Have Sources, Trees Have Roots*. Toronto: Cross Cultural Communication Centre, 1986.

Burton, Frank and Pat Carlen. *Official Discourse: On Discourse Analysis, Government Publications, Ideology and the State*. London: Routledge and Kegan Paul, 1979.

Dahlie, Jorgen and Tissa Fernando, eds. *Ethnicity, Power and Politics in Canada*. Toronto; Methuen, 1981.

Grand Council of the Mi'kmaq Nation. "The Mi'kmaq: The Covenant Chain." In Boyce Richardson, ed. *Drum Beat Anger and Renewal in Indian Country*. Toronto: Summerhill Press, 1989, pp. 71-104.

Grenville, David M. "The Role of Commission Secretary." Unpublished paper. Conference: Commissions of Inquiry: Lawyers's Values and Public Policy Makers' Values, Dalhousie Law School, February, 1988.

Hall, Stuart et al. *Policing the Crisis*. London: Macmillan, 1981.

henderson, james youngblood 'sakej'. "The Marshall Inquiry: Mi'kmaq in the Legal Consciousness." Unpublished paper, 1989.

Johnson, Eleanor V. "Mi'kmaq Tribal Consciousness in the Twentieth Century." In Stephanie Inglis, Joy Mannette and Stacey Sulewski (compilers), *Paqtatek* Volume I: Policy and Consciousness in Mi'kmaq Life. Halifax: Garamond Press, 1991.

Mannette, J.A. "' A Trial in which No One Goes to Jail': The Donald Marshall Inquiry as Hegemonic Renegotiation." *Canadian Ethnic Studies*, Special Issue on Atlantic Canada XX (3): 1988, pp. 166-80

Mannette, J.A. "'Not being a part of the way things work': Tribal culture and systemic exclusion in the Donald Marshall Inquiry." *Canadian Review of Sociology and Anthropology*, 27 (4): 1990, pp. 505-530

Marchak, M. Patricia. *Ideological Perspectives on Canada* (3rd ed.). Toronto: McGraw-Hill Ryerson, 1988.

Marshall Inquiry. MG 7A, 15, Series A (various volumes), University College of Cape Breton: Beaton Institute, 1987-1988.

Moore, Dorothy E. Multiculturalism — Ideology or Social Reality? Unpublished Ph.D. dissertation, Department of Sociology, Boston University, 1980.

Peter, Karl. "The Myth of Multiculturalism and Other Political Fables." In Jorgen Dahlie and Tissa Fernando, eds. *Ethnicity, Power and Politics in Canada*. Toronto: Methuen, 1981, pp. 56-67.

R. v. Donald Marshall, Jr. Vol II: 1971, pp. 186-93.

Royal Commission on the Donald Marshall, Jr. Prosecution *Commissioners' Report*. Halifax: Province of Nova Scotia, 1989.

Salter, Liora. "Science, Advocacy and the Media." Unpublished paper. Conference: Commissions of Inquiry: Lawyers's Values and Public Policy Makers' Values, Dalhousie Law School, February, 1988.

Salutin, Rick. *Marginal Notes*. Toronto: Lester and Orphen Dennys, 1984.

Snider, Laureen. "The Criminal Justice System." in Dennis Forcese and Stephen Richer, eds., *Social Issues* (2nd. ed.) Scarborough, Ontario: Prentice-Hall, 1988, pp. 287-320.

Sopinka, John Q.C. "The Role of Counsel to the Commission." Unpublished paper. Conference: Commissions of Inquiry: Lawyers' Values and Public Policy Makers' Values, Dalhousie Law School, February, 1988.

Taylor, Brian P. "God Was Responsible: All the Men Knew." Unpublished M.A. thesis, Department of Sociology and Anthropology, Carleton University, 1984.

Wall, Bob. "Why Donald Marshall Spent Eleven Years in Jail: Reflections on Ethnocentrism in the Criminal Justice System of Nova Scotia." Unpublished paper presented in Atlantic Canada Studies seminar, Saint Mary's University, 1988.

Whitehead, Ruth Holmes. *Stories From the Six Worlds, Micmac Legends*. Halifax: Nimbus, 1988.

Willis, Paul. "Cultural Production is Different from Cultural Reproduction is Different from Social Reproduction." Interchange, 12, 2-3: 1981, pp. 48-67.

Wildsmith, Bruce. "Submission of the Union of Nova Scotia Indians to the Royal Commission on the Donald Marshall, Jr. Prosecution." October 28, 1988.

Young, Jon, ed. *Breaking the Mosaic*. Toronto: Garamond Press, 1987.

Further Travails of Canada's Human Rights Record: The Marshall Case

M.E. Turpel/Aki-Kwe[1]

Introduction

This article scrutinizes Canada as a perceived international leader in the area of human rights protection and promotion in light of its treatment of Aboriginal peoples. In particular, the article examines human rights problems Aboriginal people face within the criminal justice system. By way of illustration, it analyses the wrongful conviction and imprisonment of Donald Marshall Jr., a Mi'kmaw whose case engaged a Royal Commission of Inquiry which released its report in early 1990. The approach taken in the Royal Commission report on Donald Marshall, Jr.'s case is critiqued in light of its failure to situate the case in broader political and cultural perspectives. In examining the alleged failures of the Royal Commission, the author implies that some major tasks lie ahead for Canada if it hopes to rectify its record of deplorable interaction with Aboriginal peoples.

> Freedom and liberty... confrontation... subjugation...resistance — all of these words describe the current situation in Nova Scotia as it relates to relations between Mi'kmaq people and our settler neighbours. Despite protections afforded by international and domestic law, a people are forcibly dispossessed of their land and resources, their governmental institutions are intentionally de-stabilized, their children condemned to a bleak future based on poverty and dependency — all so that others can reap a profit. Some backwater Third World dictatorship? No, Canada (Nova Scotia). Such has been the history of the Mi'kmaq people (Mi'kmaq Grand Council).[2]

Canada frequently claims to be an international role model with its record in the area of human rights promotion and observance. For example, the involvement of Canada in the Commonwealth vis-à-vis criticizing and calling for an end to the apartheid system in South Africa has been acclaimed as a leadership position. In many other respects, Canada strives to be at the forefront of human rights developments. It boasts a constitutionally-entrenched Charter of Rights and Freedoms,[3] a federal legislative Bill of Rights, and a plethora of statutory human rights agencies enforcing human rights standards at the federal, provincial, and territorial levels across the country. Citizens of Canada have been actively involved in international human rights initiatives, including playing a role in the drafting of the International Bill of Rights, sitting as members of the United Nations Human Rights Committee, participating in special delegations with non-governmental human rights organizations to scrutinize human rights observance in other countries, and generally speaking out on matters of international human rights concern. Canada's human rights record is often referred to as exemplary, as a continuation of a "cosmopolitan" foreign policy originating with former Prime Minister Lester B. Pearson.

Unfortunately, Canada's human rights record is one which is far from praiseworthy from the standpoint of the government behaviour towards enclaved Aboriginal peoples, which includes *Indian*, Inuit, and Metis peoples.[4] Despite growing international and domestic censure, Canada has been neither an active nor an enthusiastic promoter of the rights of Aboriginal peoples within the national political system, nor for that matter before international fora.[5]

There is very little evidence to suggest that, particularly following the 1990 army confrontations with Mohawks, the Canadian government is the least bit aware of the exigency of the Aboriginal human rights situation, the reasons for this situation, or of a process for change. Canada has become increasingly marginalized when the subject of Indigenous rights is raised in international political circles. For example, the Director of the Canadian Institute for Human Rights and Democratic Development, Ed Broadbent (former leader of the New Democratic Party of Canada) recently remarked that he would be in a particularly "...difficult position when [he] raises questions about human rights abuses in other countries... [because] these countries will be saying to me: `What about Aboriginal rights in Canada?'"[6] More and more noted international human rights activists are asking precisely that question.[7]

Canada has been found in violation of international human rights standards on two separate occasions by the United Nations Human Rights Committee because of its treatment of Aboriginal peoples, and further Indigenous complaints are pending.[8] A 1990 complaint to the Secretary-General of the United Nations by the Innu people of Labrador alleges that Canada has inflicted a consistent pattern of gross violations of human rights against them tantamount to genocide. Their communication to the Secretary-General suggests that:

> The conditions of life which Canada is inflicting upon us are calculated to bring about our destruction. Low-flying warplanes prevent us from practising our culture and religion on our land; game laws prevent us from hunting; non-recognition of our land rights prevents us from exercising our right to self-determination. Military personnel are seducing our culture. These conditions are calculated to bring about the physical destruction of the Innu people. We are losing our culture, and we are dying. Alcoholism, suicide and sickness are killing us.[9]

The Innu situation is not the exception but, rather, in the eyes of Aboriginal peoples, it is the norm. The destructive impacts of government regulation, dispossession of lands, and forced adoption of foreign cultural systems, are felt widely throughout Aboriginal communities in all regions of Canada.

Thus far, the available means of responding to this political environment in Canada have been limited for Aboriginal individuals, communities, and organizations. Formal legal institutions seem to be the only arena for discussion of the situations in which Aboriginal peoples find themselves. Aboriginal peoples have vigorously argued for protection of their rights before domestic courts with increasing, albeit tardy, costly, and unpredictable successes.[10] They have been forced to seek relief from the judiciary in light of the unwillingness of the Canadian government to negotiate land claims or other conflicts with Aboriginal peoples. As of late, even the judiciary is expressing an annoyance with the obstinate and adversarial attitude of Canadian governments in their dealings with Aboriginal peoples. Judge Barnett offered the following, in a recent decision:

> We talk about "existing aboriginal rights." But we make Indian people fight every inch of the way to achieve even the smallest victories. Some persons might question those who say this is "justice."[11]

On the rare occasions when the Canadian government has come to the negotiating table, their attitudes and approach have left Aboriginal people extremely frustrated. Rising militancy among Aboriginal people in Canada is a testimonial to the breakdown of the discussion process.

This article is about one such fight for justice by an Aboriginal person: Donald Marshall, Jr. is a Mi'kmaq person who was wrongfully convicted of murder in 1971 and served eleven years in prison before being released in 1982. His case is noteworthy as a study of racism and the inability of the Canadian legal and political system to recognize the distinct character of Aboriginal peoples (here the Mi'kmaq). Donald Marshall, Jr.'s case invites broader political and cultural analysis because not only was one individual grossly wronged by the criminal justice system but an entire political/historical relationship between two communities was compromised and ignored by government.

Donald Marshall, Jr.'s suffering is hideous. He served eleven years in prison for a murder he did not commit, beginning his sentence at the age of seventeen. In addition, he suffered almost ten additional years of public disgrace and condemnation before being publicly exonerated, vindicated, offered an apology and, finally, financially compensated for some of his losses, following the release of a Royal Commission Report into the prosecution of his case. Donald Marshall, Jr.'s case has been studied in greater detail than any case before in Canadian history. Donald Marshall, Jr. himself has given evidence at two preliminary hearings, four trials, four appeals, and three Royal Commissions of Inquiry, not to mention his involvement in several collateral legal proceedings. The Royal Commission Report is available to the reader who may not be familiar with the subtleties of the suffering of Aboriginal peoples within the Canadian legal system and for those who may be interested in comparisons with other colonial regimes.

While I would admit that Donald Marshall, Jr.'s case is an extreme one, it is not without less severe precedent in terms of Aboriginal peoples' experiences at the hands of the Canadian criminal justice system. It is a case which should be analyzed by those interested in the administration of justice and the treatment of so-called "minorities," or those interested in inter-cultural and inter-racial conflict in Canada. I would suggest that some of the critical causes of this particular miscarriage of justice have yet to be publicly examined, despite the recent Report of the Royal Commission. After providing some background to the case for those unfamiliar, it is on this latter concern which I will focus my comments.

Background to Systematic Discrimination in the Criminal Justice System

When the Royal Commission on the Donald Marshall, Jr. Prosecution (hereafter called the Marshall Commission) in January 1990 publicly released its report on the nightmare of Donald Marshall, Jr.'s wrongful conviction and imprisonment, it was touted as a momentous occasion for the Canadian criminal justice system. The criminal justice system had failed Donald Marshall, Jr. and it had to be prevented from repeating its failure. The Report contained numerous tinkering suggestions to address problems of legal process and the administration of law. However, it included only a meagre analysis of how the travesty of justice in Donald Marshall, Jr.'s case could have happened and, in particular, a poor analysis of why this happened to a Mi'kmaw.

The Royal Commission Report did acknowledge that Donald Marshall, Jr. had been wrongly convicted and imprisoned because, among other reasons, he is Mi'kmaq. This finding, which sounded like a finding of racism in the criminal justice system, was greeted with a sigh of relief on the part of members of the Aboriginal communities across the country because it supported, to a degree, what Aboriginal leaders had been strenuously arguing for years: namely, that the Canadian criminal justice system does not treat Aboriginal persons fairly and is, in fact, racist. The acknowledgement of lesser treatment based on cultural background, coming from three experienced high court justices who acted as Royal Commissioners, raised genuine cause for alarm.

Although Aboriginal leaders had been voicing dismay with the criminal justice system for years, their portrayal of the situation as racist and a product of wider systemic discrimination throughout political and legal institutions fell upon deaf ears. If it was heard, little has been done about it at an official level. It took several non-Aboriginal studies and, finally, the Royal Commission itself to provide evidence which was credible to the predominantly non-Aboriginal Canadian political and legal establishment. This is singularly a reflection on the human rights climate for Aboriginal peoples in Canada: desperate cries for help are ignored.

The official recognition of different treatment in the criminal justice system for Donald Marshall, Jr. because he was Mi'kmaq was raised only superficially in the Royal Commission Report. I view it as superficial not because it was unimportant or unhelpful, but because it was offered without cognizance of a broader definitional, ideological, cultural, and historical context for the presence of racism in the Canadian criminal justice system. Indeed, the Report shies away from the notion of racism and embraces terminology such as "different treatment" and "special position." Questions such as "what is racism?" "why is there racism in the criminal justice system?" and "where does racism in Canada come from?" were not analyzed in the Report. The notion of different treatment was raised briefly but left dangling with very little connection to the situation of Aboriginal peoples, and especially Mi'kmaq, in Canada. This can only be seen as a critical failing of the Report, indicative of a wider reluctance by officials to look racism in the face and to attempt to situate it in Canadian political life. The failure to do this in the Report has resulted in a set of recommendations which, insofar as Aboriginal people are concerned, are disconnected from Aboriginal peoples' understanding of their place in Canadian confederation and their aspirations. Not surprisingly, the Report is not a report about Aboriginal people and the criminal justice system, nor is it a report for Aboriginal people: it is a report written for the political and legal establishment, geared towards minor improvements in the justice system. This is especially unfortunate in that the Donald Marshall, Jr. case presented a perfect opportunity to look carefully at the position of Aboriginal problems in the criminal justice system and specifically to analyze racism.

That the Report even ventures toward investigation of racism or different treatment is itself a by-product of evidence which was incontrovertible. The sense that the criminal justice system treats Aboriginal people differently from non-Aboriginal people was made clear to the legal and political establishment by an important study of Aboriginal peoples and the criminal justice system by Professor Michael Jackson for the Canadian Bar Association. Jackson's report, "Locking up Natives in Canada" (Jackson: 1989), was a turning point for the legal establishment because it identified, in socio-scientific technicolour, the rampant discrimination and tragic racism in the justice system. Jackson's findings speak for themselves:

> Native people come into contact with Canada's correctional system in numbers grossly disproportionate to their representation in the community. More than any other group in Canada they are subject to the damaging impacts of the criminal justice system's heaviest sanctions. Government figures...show that almost 10 percent of the federal penitentiary population is native (including 13 percent of the federal women's prisoner population) compared to about 2 percent of the population nationally. In the west and northern parts of Canada where there are relatively high concentrations of native communities, the over-representation is more dramatic. In the Prairie region, natives make up about 5 percent of the total population but 32 percent of the penitentiary population and in the Pacific region native prisoners constitute about 12 percent of the penitentiary population while less than 5 percent of the region's general population is of native ancestry. Even more disturbing, the disproportionality is growing ... It is realistic to expect that, absent radical change, the problem will intensify due to the higher birth rate in native communities ... (Jackson: 1989, 216-217).

With data such as that compiled by Jackson, the concern about racism in the criminal justice system should have peaked for the Marshall Commission.

The year following the release of "Locking Up Natives In Canada," the Canadian Human Rights Commission, in its Annual Report, labelled the Aboriginal situation, especially Aboriginal interaction with the criminal justice system, a "national tragedy" and suggested that "the grand promise of equality of opportunity that forms the central purpose of the Canadian Human Rights Act stands in stark contrast to the conditions in which many native people live" (Commission: 1988, p. 19). The Commission expressed concern that an Aboriginal person in Canada was more likely to go to prison than to university (Commission: 1988, p. 19). In their Annual Report for the year 1989, the Canadian Human Rights Commission expressed similar concerns about the treatment of Aboriginal peoples at the hands of the Canadian criminal justice system.

While the Royal Commission on the of Donald Marshall, Jr. Prosecution was proceeding, so was a Manitoba Aboriginal Justice Inquiry, established late in 1988 in response to the killing of a prominent Winnipeg Aboriginal leader, J.J. Harper, by the Winnipeg Police Department. A later task force was established in Alberta to study the administration of justice for Aboriginal peoples in Alberta, as was an Ontario Policing study. Other studies on access to justice for "visible minorities" are in various stages of development in urban centres across Canada.

While these studies and inquiries have called into question the administration of justice in a dramatic way, they are simply the tip of the iceberg from an Aboriginal perspective. The identification of systematic racism is just the start of an arduous and painful process of bringing into public view serious human rights failings on the part of Canada. However, there appears to be a reluctance, at an official state level, to do more than simply hint about the existence of a problem with racism or systemic discrimination in the justice system. There is little commitment to understanding racism, its antecedents, or its effects on Aboriginal people. Just the notion of identifying racism has been a difficult process for non-Aboriginal people. Indeed, the deliberations and findings of the various special studies have been greeted with backlash and hostility when officials, especially police, have been questioned with respect to their attitudes toward Aboriginal people.[12] The government has made no effort here to step in and take a leadership role in preventing or containing backlashes against the Aboriginal community.

The incidence of discrimination in the criminal justice system is widespread, as the studies show. As can be imagined with the incarceration rates listed above, there are far too many cases and incidents to detail here. The most memorable case for Canadians for some time to come will likely be that of Donald Marshall, Jr. Even apart from consideration of discrimination, his case stands as a great travesty of justice in that he was wrongfully convicted of murder, the penultimate Canadian criminal offence, and his case is instructive for a study of racism and incompetence in the Canadian justice system.

How Donald Marshall, Jr., his family, and Mi'kmaq people endured the injustices inflicted upon him by the Canadian state, will never be fully known.[13] As the eldest son of the Grand Chief of the Mi'kmaq Grand Council (the spiritual and political leader of the Mi'kmaq Nation), his ordeal affected his entire community. Moreover, the broader political implications of the case, given Donald Marshall, Jr.'s family status in a closely knit kinship community are understandably profound. Unfortunately, this connection seemed largely lost on the Commissioners in their Report.

The Aboriginal experience of institutionalized racism in Canada, resulting in a web of mistrust of non-Aboriginal officials, is one which flies in the face of a legal system theoretically premised on the rule of law and equal access to justice. It is frequently said that the rule of law is the soul of the modern state. If so, Donald Marshall, Jr.'s case should provoke considerable soul-searching. Aboriginal perspectives on the criminal justice system in Canada reflect concerns which one would expect to find in South Africa, El Salvador, or elsewhere, not in an ostensibly "progressive" Western liberal democracy such as Canada.

Aboriginal families in Canada do not feel secure that they will be treated fairly by the criminal justice system and are not willing to accept a future which will involve the incarceration of a large number of their children. What can Aboriginal parents expect for their children? Will their future hold anything more, in effect, than their parents' experiences of forced assimilation at residential schools, or their treatment at the hands of the Canadian government which prohibited ceremonies and banned spiritual practices?

The State Wrong Against Donald Marshall, Jr.

The events of the Donald Marshall, Jr. Case are well known in Canada. For those unfamiliar with the facts, a detailed reconstruction of them is available in the Royal Commission Report, *Digest of Findings*. I sketch only an overview here of the facts and critical comments on them by the Commissioners. On May 28, 1971, a young Black man, Sandy Seale, was murdered in a park in Sydney, Nova Scotia. Sydney is in Cape Breton,

Nova Scotia, the area of the Canadian Atlantic provinces most densely populated by Mi'kmaq. Accompanying him in the park was Donald Marshall, Jr., a seventeen-year-old Mi'kmaw who was injured in the events which led to the murder of his acquaintance. Mr. Seale's death and Mr. Marshall's injury were inflicted by Roy Ebsary, a caucasian fifty-nine-year-old former ship's cook who was described to the Royal Commission as drunk and dangerous (Marshall Commission: 1989, Vol. 1, 2).

From the outset, the police response to the stabbings in the park was unprofessional, inadequate, and incompetent. Police officers did not conduct a thorough investigation and the Sergeant of Detectives on the case suspected very shortly after the event that Donald Marshall, Jr. was the murderer. The Sergeant of Detectives did not take seriously Donald Marshall, Jr.'s voluntary statements and assistance to the police about the events in the park or his co-operation with them because "he considered Marshall a troublemaker and ... he shared what we [the Commissioners] believe was a general sense in Sydney's white community at the time that Indians were not worth as much as whites" (Marshall Commission: 1989, Vol. 1, 3).

The Sergeant of Detective's investigation of the murder was directed at building a case against Donald Marshall, Jr. In pursuit of this goal, he influenced witnesses and even accepted the evidence of an unstable sixteen year old eyewitness who was known to "fantasize and invent stories to make himself the centre of attention" (Marshall Commission: 1989, Vol. 1, 3). The Royal Commission Report found that the fact that Marshall was Mi'kmaq was one important reason why Sergeant MacIntyre singled him out so quickly as the prime suspect without evidence to support his conclusion (Marshall Commission: 1989, Vol. 1, 41). They found that MacIntyre's conviction as to Marshall's guilt dominated his conduct of the investigation and committed it to a course that was designed to select only evidence to support his theory, thus ignoring other relevant information about the actual scenario. This closed-minded approach on his part, stubbornly pursued, led to a flawed investigation, culminating in the laying of charges against Marshall for the murder of his acquaintance (Marshall Commission: 1989, Vol. 1, 41). Sergeant MacIntyre did not tell the truth to the Royal Commission on the Donald Marshall, Jr. Prosecution when he denied speaking to witnesses and influencing them with respect to their statements (Marshall Commission: 1989, Vol. 1, 47).

The Commissioners found that both the crown prosecutor and defence counsel in the Marshall Case similarly failed to discharge their obligations adequately or properly and that the trial judge failed to interpret correctly doctrines of evidence law, with the result that the trial process was flawed and Donald Marshall, Jr. wrongfully convicted. The crown prosecutor did not make the necessary effort to find out the reasons for conflicting witness statements, nor did he disclose the existence of earlier contradictory statements by witnesses to Marshall's defence counsel (Marshall Commission: 1989, Vol. 1, 72). Moreover, Donald Marshall, Jr.'s own counsel let him down at numerous points in failing to put forth a complete and vigilant defence. These actions and inactions were found by the Commissioners to be the antithesis of the conduct expected from competent, skilled legal counsel (Marshall Commission: 1989, Vol. 1, 73).

The fact that Donald Marshall, Jr. was Mi'kmaq evidently influenced the level of representation he received. Indeed, the fact that he was Mi'kmaq emerges as the connecting thread in the pattern of incompetency that became the reconstructed Donald Marshall, Jr. Case in the Royal Commission Report. While the Commissioners hedged on calling this racism, not attempting to explicate why Donald Marshall, Jr.'s being Mi'kmaq prejudiced his representation, it is the most haunting matter of the whole affair.

After Donald Marshall, Jr.'s trial, when new evidence on the case was brought to police attention in 1971, a shockingly poor reconsideration of the case was undertaken. The new evidence was not taken seriously, nor were problems in the case fully explored. The Royal Commissioners found that there can be no doubt that this incompetent re-investigation in 1971 was a major contributing factor to Donald Marshall, Jr. spending eleven years in jail for a crime he did not commit, instead of a much shorter period. The reason for the poor investigation was deemed to be a blindness on the part of the officers as to their assumptions about Donald Marshall, Jr.'s character (Marshall Commission: 1989, Vol. 1, 83).

Donald Marshall, Jr.'s 1972 appeal of his conviction was also problematic, in that the Crown, the defence and the police failed to recognize, in advance, arguments on the serious evidentiary errors involved in Donald Marshall, Jr.'s trial. His defence counsel failed to argue certain issues at the appeal which represented, in the Commissioners' view, a serious breach of the standard of professional conduct expected and required of defence counsel (Marshall Commission: 1989, Vol. 1, 85). Moreover, the Attorney General's Department treated Donald Marshall, Jr.'s 1972 appeal as routine and failed to raise errors in the law not raised by the defence, even though they had a professional responsibility to do so (Marshall Commission: 1989, Vol. 1, 86). This failure contributed to the denial of Marshall's appeal of his wrongful conviction and resulted in his continued incarceration. The Royal Commission found that a Court of Appeal has a duty to review the record of a criminal case placed before it and to raise any significant errors with counsel and ensure that it is properly argued: a duty not performed in Donald Marshall, Jr.'s case.

While Donald Marshall, Jr. was in prison, first at a maximum security institution, later at a lower security institution, members of Donald Marshall, Jr.'s prison case management team placed immense pressure on him to admit that he was guilty of murdering Mr. Seale. Later in his sentence, a request for a pass to go home for Christmas was declined because he refused to acknowledge his guilt, thereby refusing, in their view, to take responsibility for his crime. They saw his declaration of guilt as the only road to "recovery." Yet he was innocent. The effect of the Canadian corrections policy concerning prisoners' claims of innocence is that a prisoner claiming innocence has a more difficult battle in obtaining early release. Donald Marshall, Jr.'s reaction to the pressure on him to admit his guilt caused him immense frustration and deep psychological and emotional scars. It ultimately provoked aggressive behaviour while in prison (Marshall Commission: 1989, Vol. 1, 110).

When a Reference to the Nova Scotia Court of Appeal was requested by the Federal Minister of Justice in 1983, following a more competent review of Donald Marshall, Jr.'s conviction and casting doubt on his involvement in the murder (particularly after he contacted police to let them know that the real murderer had written to him in prison), Chief Justice MacKeigan of the Nova Scotia Court of Appeal influenced officials in the Department of Justice with respect to the determination of the final form of the Reference so that the Reference was constituted under a section of the Canadian Criminal Code which shifted the onus to Marshall to prepare and prove his own innocence, as opposed to the Crown bearing the responsibility of showing why it had misled the court (Marshall Commission: 1989, Vol. 1, 115). Moreover, one of the Justices sitting on the Appeal, Mr. Justice Pace, was the Attorney General at the time of the original trial and appeal. The Commissioners concluded that he should not have sat as a member of the panel hearing the Appeal.

When the Court of Appeal in the Reference finally quashed Donald Marshall, Jr.'s conviction and entered a verdict of acquittal, they made several gratuitous comments which were troubling. They suggested that Donald Marshall, Jr. had "admittedly" committed perjury and that his "untruthfulness contributed in large measure to his conviction." The Royal Commission found that the Court of Appeal, in acquitting Donald Marshall, Jr., made a serious and fundamental error by placing the blame on him for the wrong committed by the state. The Court of Appeal Justices commented on the case with respect to perjury and to the effect that any miscarriage of justice in Donald Marshall, Jr.'s Case was more imagined that real, and that, in any event, he was responsible for any injustice done because he had lied and was attempting to commit a robbery on the night of the murder. These comments haunted Marshall like a demon following the Reference decision, surfacing regularly in the press and seriously prejudicing his ability to seek compensation for the wrongs perpetrated against him. They were warm comfort for those who self-righteously denied a miscarriage of justice had occurred. These accusations also fit comfortably within popular racist stereotypes of *Indians*. *Indians* were, in effect, written off as liars, thieves, drunks, in other words, "savages." Just as MacIntyre had a preconceived theory of Donald Marshall, Jr.'s guilt based on his racist stereotype of the Mi'kmaq, apparently so too did the court.

The Commissioners found that the panel of judges took it upon themselves to "pronounce" Marshall guilty of an offence — attempted robbery — with which he was never charged. One of the cardinal principles of the Canadian criminal justice system, which is constitutionally enshrined, is the notion that an individual is innocent until proven guilty. Not only was Donald Marshall, Jr. entitled to be presumed innocent but, in this case, he had not even been charged with theft. Moreover, the Court of Appeal failed to deal with the key problems of the case in their decision, such as the failure of the Crown to disclose evidence, especially conflicting statements by witnesses, to defence counsel (Marshall Commission: 1989, Vol. 1, 121). Instead, they treated the case as routine. The consequence of the Court of Appeal's gratuitous comments in the Reference decision was that the blame was placed squarely on Donald Marshall, Jr.'s shoulders for his wrongful conviction. The decision amounted, in the Commissioners' view, to a defence of the criminal justice system at his expense. Even in the narrowest sense, the Commissioners found that Donald Marshall Jr.'s wrongful imprisonment for eleven years in a federal penitentiary can only be seen as a miscarriage of justice in the extreme (Marshall Commission: 1989, Vol.1, 125).

Following the Royal Commission Report, another chapter in the case was opened when a public Canadian Judicial Council panel was constituted to consider the appropriateness of the Appeal Court judges' behaviours in the 1983 Reference decision. The Justices, who were unwilling to participate in the Royal Commission, came prepared to fight at this Inquiry, stubbornly reiterating their offensive comments through their legal counsel. Once again, they failed to acknowledge the injustice done to Donald Marshall, Jr., an innocent seventeen-year-old boy, and obstinately hid behind their prejudices.

Critique of the Royal Commission Findings and Recommendations

The Royal Commissioners' principal finding in their report on the Donald Marshall, Jr. Prosecution was that a two-tier system of justice exists in Nova Scotia — a system that responds differently depending on the status, wealth, and race of the person investigated (Marshall Commission: 1989, Vol. 1, 220). Donald Marshall Jr., as a Mi'kmaw, was on the bottom of the second tier. In effect, there was no justice for him in Nova Scotia. The Commissioners concluded that the Canadian criminal justice system had failed Donald Marshall, Jr. "at virtually every turn," from his arrest and wrongful conviction in 1971 up to — and even beyond — his acquittal by the Court of Appeal in the Reference decision in 1983. The tragedy of this failure was, in their view, exacerbated by clear evidence that this miscarriage of justice could have, and should have, been prevented or at least corrected quickly, if those involved in the system had carried out their duties in a professional and/or competent manner (Marshall Commission: 1989, Vol. 1, 15). The reason that they did not do so was, at least in part, because Marshall is Mi'kmaq, and therefore, a non-priority in the Canadian criminal justice system.

The Marshall Commission Report made eighty-two recommendations with respect to the administration of criminal justice, eleven of which were specifically aimed at addressing the difficulties Mi'kmaq people face in the criminal justice system. These include recommendations directed at increasing the representation of Mi'kmaq in administrative positions in the criminal justice system (as police officers, etc.); an improved legal aid system; a pilot-project "Native Criminal Court," with limited summary conviction jurisdiction; cultural awareness training for judges, lawyers, and police; improved access to legal education for Mi'kmaq, and a political forum on Aboriginal justice issues. It is significant that the Report made no recommendations as to the laying of criminal charges against those officials involved in the suppression of evidence or the obstruction of justice in the handling of this case through its various developments. In addition, the Report did not comment on the inaction or ignorance of the federal and provincial politicians in responding to this miscarriage of justice.

The Report recommendations were formed with little direct consultation with the Mi'kmaq community. While the Union of Nova Scotia Indians had standing at the Inquiry, they were clearly seen as marginal to the process. In fact, many of the recommendations are contrary to submissions by Mi'kmaq. For example, there is Dr. Marie Battiste, a highly respected Mi'kmaq educator who, with sakej henderson, a legal advisor to the Mi'kmaq Grand Council, prepared a powerful statement appended to Volume 3 of the Report, the Research Study on *The Mi'kmaq and Criminal Justice in Nova Scotia*. This statement seems to have been ignored. Dr. Battiste's submission provides the needed historical, political, and cultural context of the Report. Unfortunately, this context was not reflected in the recommendations in any meaningful way.

From an Aboriginal viewpoint, the Report contains several positive elements. These include the vindication of Donald Marshall, Jr. and the official recognition that different standards of treatment are institutionalized in the Canadian justice system. The Report did not satisfy many people in the Aboriginal community because it did not recognize Donald Marshall, Jr.'s status in the Mi'kmaq community. As noted earlier, he is the eldest son of the late Grand Chief, the political and spiritual leader of the Nation. The Commissioners did not recognize this, nor did they appreciate the immense stigma this wrongful conviction and imprisonment left in the whole Mi'kmaq community as a result.

Probably the most striking, although largely undeveloped, statement or suggestion in the Report was the comment by the Commissioners that:

> In our view, Native Canadians have the right to a justice system that they respect and which has respect for them, and which dispenses justice in a manner consistent with and sensitive to their history, culture and language (Marshall Commission: 1989, Digest of Findings and Recommendations, 11).

The Report did not, apart from this statement, consider what kind of justice system Aboriginal peoples could respect, nor did they consider what type(s) of structures could, from an Aboriginal perspective, dispense justice in a manner consistent with Aboriginal histories, cultures, and languages. The recommendation that a Native Criminal Court be established with limited Canadian summary conviction jurisdiction was included as a compromising suggestion by the Commissioners in meeting this goal. There is no evidence to suggest that a Native Criminal Court would be an institution to be respected by the Mi'kmaq or one which was sensitive to Mi'kmaq language, history, or culture. Indeed, the terms "*their* history, culture, and language" in the quotation excerpted above, reveal the Commissioners' ignorance regarding the diversity of peoples who are the First Peoples of what is now "Canada." There is no single language, history, or culture.

In this regard, the two greatest failings of the Report's recommendations are that they do not make the connections which one must make to understand the context of this case, and they are not rooted in a consensus from the Mi'kmaq community about what type of a justice system can nurture respect. The political, ideological and cultural context of Mi'kmaq-Canadian relations and how they have been affected by this case were not considered by the Commissioners. Relatedly, the reasons for racism in the criminal justice system, especially from an historical perspective in Canada, were not explored in the Report. To take the second issue first, one must understand that racism does not exist in a vacuum. The context of colonialization and broader subjugation of Aboriginal peoples by the British, French, and later "Canadian" states is the antecedent of its appearance in an institutionalized form in the criminal justice system. One of the compelling points of the Jackson study, referred to earlier, is that it accurately identifies the experience of colonialism, of wrongful dispossession of Aboriginal lands, of cultural hegemony, and of state-sanctioned religious proselytization, as the basis for systematic racial discrimination in the criminal justice system. Donald Marshall, Jr.'s experiences can only be understood in this light. Jackson argues that:

> What links ... views of native criminality as caused by poverty or alcohol is the historical process which native people have experienced in Canada, along with Indigenous people in other parts of the world — the process of colonization. In the Canadian context that process, with the advance first of the agricultural and then the industrial frontier, has left native people in most parts of the country dispossessed of all but the remnants of what was once their homelands; that process, superintended by missionaries and Indian agents armed with power of the law, took such extreme forms as criminalizing central Indian institutions such as the potlatch and sun dance, and systematically undermined the foundations of many native communities. The native people of Canada have, over the course of the last two centuries, been moved to the margins of their own territories and of our "just" society ... (Jackson: 1988, 216).

The Royal Commission Report on the Donald Marshall, Jr. Prosecution does not explore these links. While Jackson attended a consultation meeting with the Commissioners, his arguments, not to mention those of Mi'kmaq presenters such as Dr. Battiste, did not connect. Perhaps the Commissioners were naive or felt constricted in their reporting, or maybe these connections were too painful to confront, too difficult to navigate — too "political" for judges. The Report steps into the messy matter of racism by hinting at different treatment and by requesting a special study on Mi'kmaq and criminal justice which included a Mi'kmaq perspective.

However, the background study, and specifically the submissions by Mi'kmaq appended to that document (Volume 3) did not work their way into the Commission recommendations.

Links between racism and colonialism are the roots of the tragedy of the criminal justice system in its application to Aboriginal people. Aboriginal peoples have been dispossessed of their lands, have been made the wards of a Big Brother state, and are alienated from the dominant legal and political system. Aboriginal political structures are not considered part of Canada — they are repressed, ignored, or trivialized by the state. Not surprisingly, interactions with the criminal justice system are more frequent and must be seen as moments of a more tragic and pervasive logic of domination and repression of Aboriginal peoples. Given that the mandate of the Royal Commission was to investigate how this tragedy occurred and to make recommendations to prevent future tragedies from happening, it is unfortunate that an exposure of these links was not vigorously pursued by the Commissioners. Perhaps it was, though, courageous enough just to identify racism, rather than risk overwhelming the public by analyzing it. Courageous as it might have been, it missed the bigger point.

Institutionalized racism for Aboriginal people is a by-product of colonization, of the forced imposition of an alien legal, political, and cultural regime onto communities. Colonialism has inflicted its own economic logic, a supporting ideological baggage of paternalism, assumptions of superiority, and liberal belief in the progress of "mankind" as an organic and undifferentiated whole. In the so-called New World, colonialism involved dispossession of Aboriginal homelands, repression of cultural and spiritual rituals, removal of children from their homes, renaming families with European names, re-education in a European system, and treaty promises and agreements which have been broken and ignored. Aboriginal peoples have not been part of the internationally monitored decolonization process or trusteeship program. They are trapped in larger, consuming states. This has resulted in a desperate preoccupying struggle for maintenance of Aboriginal peoples' existence in the face of the imposition of powerful ideological systems and use of state force to repress differences. In a Western liberal democratic state, based on the rule of law, and other charged organizing principles, this has produced a two-faces-of-Janus state — or rather one face with a mask — the equality-seeking liberal democratic mask and the deeply repressive and hegemonic face. What the Mi'kmaq see and what non-Aboriginal people see in the institutionalized arrangements of political ideals in Canada are effectively different faces. They live in different worlds. For the Mi'kmaq, colonization has involved, in Dr. Battiste's submission, the following face:

> To the Mi'kmaq, all the provincial conceptions of law witness a structure of racial dominion. All provincial authority seems mere prejudices of another era, a colonial society where racial whim produced political arrangements for which no independent justification can be found. Every judicial case concerning aboriginal and treaty forces judges to decide, at least implicitly, which of the competing sets of beliefs and sovereign commands in society should be given priority . . . Being enclosed in this environment accounts for a basic, common experience of Mi'kmaq behaviours that would otherwise remain unintelligible; the sense of being surrounded by injustice without knowing where justice lies (Marshall Report 1989, Vol. 3, 98).

Identifying racism in the manner that the Royal Commission Report did is a classic instance of superficiality. The identification of racism in the criminal justice system, apart from the greater context, is a case of just seeing the tree when a forest surrounds. It is the historical process of colonization, supported by a repressive liberal ideology (enforced by the state) which is the forest. Donald Marshall, Jr. was not singled out as a murderer instead of a seventeen-year-old victim of an assault simply because he was Mi'kmaq — it was because of what being Mi'kmaq means to state officials in the ideological context of colonialism: it means being presumed to be inferior, unworthy, untrustworthy, a savage, a liar, and a thief. It means being a member of a sub-class. As Dr. Battiste explains: "Because we [Mi'kmaq] are the underclass in Canadian society, our visibility is low, political resistance minimal, . . . the incentive for the majority to take advantage of legal discrimination to confiscate our wealth has been great" (Marshall Report: 1989, Vol. 3, 101-102]).

Flowing from this, I would suggest that a second general failing of the Report was its failure to take notice of, or express as part of its recommendations, an appreciation of the particular historical relationship between Mi'kmaq people and the Canadian state and especially the failure to incorporate an analysis of the Treaty of Peace and Friendship of 1752 into their recommendations. The Mi'kmaq have a special compact with the Crown, the Elekewaki (In the King's House) Compact, rooted in a 1752 Treaty with the English, and further accession treaties (1752-1779). This Treaty of 1752, as the central agreement between the English and the Mi'kmaq on a range of topics, including an article (Article 8) on conflicts between Mi'kmaq and non-Mi'kmaq, is seen as the foundation of a relationship based on the meeting of minds of two peoples and the international notion of *pacta sunt sevanda*. The Treaty has been recognized by the Supreme Court of Canada as validly in force and as enshrining legal commitments to be solemnly respected (*Simon v. The Queen* [1985] 2 S.C.R. 387).

The Elekewaki Compact was silent on issues of criminal justice. For the Mi'kmaq, this is interpreted to mean that pre-existing tribal authority for criminal law is continued. Therefore, for them, the Donald Marshall, Jr. Case represents an affront of two varieties: first, the removal of a Mi'kmaq child in a manner inconsistent with the principles and procedures of Canadian criminal law; and secondly, the illegitimate and unilateral assumption of authority by Canada over a Mi'kmaw contrary to the Elekewaki Compact. As Dr. Battiste explains:

> The Grand Council perceives the tribal-Crown relationship as one between sovereigns, based on treaty and negotiation, and rooted in the exclusive fiduciary responsibility that the Federal Government has to the Mi'kmaw Nation. From this perspective, the Council perceives it has an existing aboriginal right to provide for administration of justice under the Federal Criminal Code for all Mi'kmaw and in all Lands reserved for them. These pre-existing rights were never delegated to the Crown in any Treaty, thus it is still reserved to the Council under our constitutionally protected aboriginal rights. This is not a startling discovery in Canada. Canadian federalism consists of a constellation of governments, rather than an association of individuals held together by a single government (Marshall Report: 1989, Vol. 3, 99).

The Royal Commission Report failed to analyze the particular historical/political relationship between the Mi'kmaq and the Crown in criminal justice matters. This makes their Report stand out as an historical, from an Aboriginal view, denial of the legal-historical context for Mi'kmaq/British relations. It reveals the limited perspective of those within the dominant legal system even to acknowledge their own political obligations and to consider the implications of these treaty obligations for the Donald Marshall, Jr. Case. Moreover, it means that certain recommendations of the Commissioners, such as the recommendations for a Native Criminal Court trying summary convictions under the Criminal Code, are inappropriate because this is a further imposition of an alien regime, even in the face of commitments to a justice system Aboriginal people can "respect." This is not a recommendation based on the Elekewaki Compact, or a negotiated agreement for addressing injustice in the legal and political system. This type of recommendation reflects an ignorance of an historical relationship and reveals the limitations of the Commissioners in understanding the roots of racism. From an Aboriginal perspective, it indicates that even those "sympathetic" or "courageous" enough to identify that there are problems for Aboriginal peoples in the Canadian criminal justice system cannot transcend their particular cultural and political context to appreciate where these problems fit into an historical relationship. This appreciation is tied to any possible reconciliation.

Conclusions

Perhaps it is too early to assess the response of the non-Aboriginal community to the Royal Commission Report. At the six-month point after the Report's release, the federal and provincial governments were criticized for inaction on practically all recommendations affecting Aboriginal peoples.[14] The Nova Scotia government initially responded quickly to the Royal Commission Report, accepting in principle most recommendations. However, implementation of these has progressed at a snail's pace, if at all. The federal government has yet to offer a written response to the Report.

One preliminary note on the Royal Commission Report by a non-Aboriginal legal scholar voiced concern with the Report. Professor Archie Kaiser cautions:

> The rule of law and equality before the law are still worth striving for, but they are not concepts which should be considered in the depoliticized atmosphere which the authors of the Commission Report seem to prefer. These are highly charged symbols the meaning of which can be manipulated for good and evil in a society which is much in need of change, as seen from the perspective of the Marshall debacle. *There is grave danger in letting the beneficent liberal idealism of the Report overcome the visceral sense of revulsion stimulated by the Marshall case.* Worship at the feet of a rule of law icon is encouraged by the Report, but there are strong reasons for not being satisfied with isolated or formalistic changes contained within the criminal justice system (Kaiser: 1990, p. 374, emphasis added).

For Aboriginal people, the danger of post-Marshall damage control in the name of the rule of law may mean the continuation of a colonial ideological mentality: the imposition of one legal system upon another, the repression of Indigenous law and spirituality, and the dishonour of the Elekewaki Compact of 1752. Law is, in fact, far more differentiated culturally and ideologically than the liberal conception of the rule of law doctrine imagines. Yet, conceptually, it is not understood as a rule of laws.

In a colonial context, it is never possible to speak of law in the singular — there are only laws. Perhaps it is only legitimate to speak of lawyers. The notion of fostering the respect of Mi'kmaq for and by the criminal justice system is one which requires a recognition of legal pluralism and an awareness of the cultural locality of the criminal justice system and its administrators. Recommendations which cannot embrace this notion do little but save face for the dominant legal system and obviate the need for profound change. Consequently, when the Commissioners recommend the establishment of a pilot-project, summary-conviction Native Criminal Court on a Mi'kmaq reserve, enforcing exclusively Canadian law (not Mi'kmaq or tribal law), they fail to realize that this just makes the sense of injustice seem closer to home. What is required is something more respectful of Mi'kmaq norms. As Dr. Battiste articulated in her submission, "[c]ultural values do not sustain themselves; they require sustenance from tribal structures. Tribal courts can sustain the best of our cultural values in a modern context . . ." (Marshall Report: 1989, Vol. 3, 101). The Royal Commission Report contains no recommendations aimed at sustaining or reinvigorating tribal structures or the cultural and social foundation of the Mi'kmaq community. In this respect, it failed both Donald Marshall, Jr. and his people. It neglects to see the more complex reasons for this tragedy while issuing recommendations directed at perfecting a colonialist legal regime which is more the cause than the solution to the problem; the disease and not the doctor.

The Canadian criminal justice system did fail Donald Marshall, Jr. and the Mi'kmaq people. It fails all Aboriginal people in various, albeit perhaps not as dramatic, ways. The most basic rights to human dignity and the collective right to be respected as different peoples (call it self-determination or self-preservation) have been denied to Aboriginal peoples in Canada. As a result, Aboriginal peoples inhabit the margins of the "just" Canadian society. Until the reasons for this status are more fully acknowledged and accepted, and steps are taken to address fundamental issues such as land claims and dispossession, it is absurd to hold Canada out to be an international leader in the field of human rights.

The Marshall Commission Report similarly does not deserve accolades. While it acknowledged errors, negligence, and mismanagement, it did not make the connections necessary to begin the process of developing a dialogue about a justice system that Aboriginal peoples can respect, or which respects Aboriginal peoples. It deflected attention elsewhere and appeased shallow guilt feelings. This is not a way out of the suffering Donald Marshall, Jr. endured; for Aboriginal peoples, it is simply a further neglect of the disease. It is not the end to racism, but a more subtle packaging of it.

One can only hope that the other justice inquiries underway, such as the Manitoba Aboriginal Justice Inquiry, will tackle racism in the justice system in a way that embraces an understanding of what racism is and why it exists in Canada, and will provide suggestions of a process to get away from institutionalized racism. Otherwise, participants will be conducting elaborate exercises in institutional and doctrinal face-saving.

Notes

[1] Assistant Professor, Dalhousie Law School; Member, Indigenous Bar Association. I would like to dedicate this article to a friend and fellow member of the Indigenous Bar Association, Shirley Olson, who died suddenly in the summer of 1990 on the steps of the Manitoba legislature, while she was participating in a protest against Canadian government treatment of Mohawks.

[2] From B. Richardson, ed., *Drumbeat: Anger and Renewal in Indian Country* (Toronto: Summerhill Press, 1988) pp. 73-74.

[3] For a critical perspective on the Canadian Charter of Rights and Freedoms, see M.E. Turpel, "Aboriginal Peoples and The Canadian Charter: Interpretive Monopolies, Cultural Differences" (1989-90)*Canadian Human Rights Yearbook*

[4] I use the term "Aboriginal" throughout this article to refer to the First Peoples of Canada which includes all tribes such as Cree, Mohawk, Dene, and the Metis, or mixed ancestry First Nations/French people, and the Inuit, formerly pejoratively labelled "Eskimos."

[5] For example, at the 1990 session of the United Nations Sub-Commission on the Prevention of Discrimination and Protection of Minorities, Canada failed to submit its reports, which were particularly important on aspects of international human rights observance in the area of Indigenous peoples' situation.

[6] Reported in P. Poirer, "Broadbent Assails Use of Food as Weapon in Oka Dispute," *Globe and Mail*, 24 July, 1990, p. A4.

[7] Bishop Desmond Tutu's visit to Canada in August 1990, and specifically his stay at a Northern Ontario *Indian* Reserve, led to his making several highly critical statements about Canada's human rights role in this area. Jesse Jackson had also visited Canada in 1990 with a view to appraising the situation at Kanesatake.

[8] See, *Lovelace* v. *Canada*, (1981) Report of the Human Rights Committee, GAOR 36th Sess., Supp. No. 40 (A/36/40), Annex XVIII, 166; and, *Ominayak* v. *Canada*, U.N. Doc. CCPR/C/38/ID/167/1984, released 28 March 1990. See also a third

ruling (on admissibility) which portends another violation of international human rights law: *Mi'kmaq Tribal Society* v. *Canada* CCPR/C/39/D/205/1986, released 21 August 1990.

[9] Innu complaint against Canada pursuant to UN Resolution 1503, 20 March 1990, acknowledged 31 May 1990, U.N. Doc. G/SO 215/1 CANA., p. 12.

[10] See the Supreme Court of Canada decision in *Sparrow* v. *R.* [1990] 3 C.N.L.R. 146.

[11] *R.* v. *Archie* [1989] 4 C.N.L.R. 114 (B.C. Prov. Ct.).

[12] This was particularly evident during the deliberations of the Manitoba Aboriginal Justice Committee following the suicide of one of the investigating officers.

[13] There is a book written about Donald Marshall Jr.'s experience which is factually descriptive although not his account. It is the account of Canadian journalist, M. Harris, *Justice Denied: The Law Versus Donald Marshall* (Toronto: Totem Books, 1986). The book was also made into a film, produced by Paul Cowan, which is available through the National Film Board of Canada. Perhaps for fear of legal reprisals, the film avoids focusing on racism.

[14] Union of Nova Scotia Indians Press Release, 3 August 1990.

References

Canadian Bar Association Native Justice Committee Report, *Aboriginal Rights in Canada: An Agenda for Action*. Ottawa: The Canadian Bar Association, 1988.

Canadian Human Rights Commission, Annual Report. Ottawa: Government of Canada Printers, 1988, 1989.

Commission of Inquiry Concerning the Adequacy of Compensation Paid to Donald Marshall, Jr. Halifax: Government of the Province of Nova Scotia, June 1990.

Jackson, M. "Locking up Natives in Canada." 23 *U.B.C.L.Rev.*,1989, p. 215.

Kaiser, H.A. "The Aftermath of the Marshall Commission: A Preliminary Opinion." 13 *Dalhousie Law Journal*, 1990, p. 364.

Little Rock, "The American Indian in the White Man's Prisons: A Story of Genocide." 2 *Journal of Prisoners on Prisons*, 1989, p.1.

Mi'kmaw Chiefs, "The Covenant Chain," in B. Richardson, ed., *Drumbeat: Anger and Renewal in Indian Country*. Toronto: Summerhill Press, 1989.

Mi'kmaq Response to the Report of the Royal Commission on the Donald Marshall, Jr. Prosecution. Unpublished: Union of Nova Scotia Indians, 21 February, 1990.

Royal Commission on the Donald Marshall, Jr., Prosecution. Halifax: Government of the Province of Nova Scotia, 1989.

Sugar, F., and L. Fox. "Nitsum Peyako Seht'wawinlskwewak: Breaking Chains" 3 *Canadian Journal of Women and the Law*, 1989-90, p. 465.

Turpel, M.E. "Aboriginal Peoples and the Canadian Charter: Interpretive Monopolies, Cultural Differences." *Canadian Human Rights Yearbook*, 1989-90, p. 4.

Beyond the Marshall Inquiry: An Alternative Mi'kmaq Worldview and Justice System
Kjikeptin[1] Alex Denny

In the Mi'kmaq worldview, individual behaviour faithfully accommodates collective culture; there is a firm consensus of proper respect of inherent dignities. The mechanism by which individual passions are prevented from wreaking havoc on society is deference to shared values, reinforced by family opinion and rewarded with honour and respect. Order in society presupposes and evokes order in the soul. Order is a matter of kinship, education, and personal self-control. Every family is equal and every Mi'kmaw has an equal right to be heard and heeded by others. Coercive institutions are generally absent, if not vigorously opposed. Aggressiveness is considered wrongful and contrary to human dignity.

Like other Indigenous worldviews, the Mi'kmaq only recognizes binding obligations which arise from consent. The most striking trait of the consensual order is the almost exclusive commitment to custom or interactional law. Written laws, codes, and regulations are still unknown, and imposed authoritative systems are kept within strictest limits. To codify customary forms of behaviour or law is to destroy the living flexibility that is their greatest virtue.

Mi'kmaq could violate the spiritual order. But their violations are not seen as derived from a concept of wrongness. The idea of change creates an understanding of mistakes and conflicts. Violating the harmony of the natural order unleashes dangerous forces both in the spiritual and social realms, which articulate a conflict. Being Mi'kmaq means the ability to withdraw from conflict and to think good thoughts.

Traditionally, the very fact of seeking a "political" solution to a situation was cause for concern. Most problems were resolved with the extended family, not by the Mawi'omi or district chiefs. Solutions were likewise spontaneous and contextual, not based on logical reasoning, rules, or trying to control events. Instead, like the ecosystem, resolutions were the shortest paths back to equilibrium, which depended entirely on the circumstances in each case. Usually, the families were satisfied with whatever solution presented itself—happy that the conflict was over and harmony restored. Harmony, not justice, is the ideal.

There is no concept of an "innocent" or "guilty" individual. The priority is not determining culpability, but resolving the conflict quickly to maintain harmony. If the offender repents and wishes to make peace, an exchange of presents and other suitable atonements takes away bad feeling and restores good thoughts.

This order can be described as a system of *relational* standards of conduct, based on environmental integrity and human dignity. No one person could make laws; they were a product of living together, and consent and understanding. Customary law is a process of reconciliation based on shared examples or models of conduct. It is regarded by the Indigenous mind as a spiritual force, like instinct to the animal world and gravity to the scientific community. It evolved from oral traditions, the daily traditions of sharing hardship and joy with each other. They were renewed nightly over the campfire by lengthy discussion of their experiences; today the same process is often carried on at the supper table. It is an empirically-based study of human behaviour, extremely critical and moral in its nature. At the same time, it is celebratory, expressive, and performative. Its scope is not limited to humans, but also includes all things and spirits in nature. The result is a strong community of shared obligations, in which obedience is a natural result of understanding. This understanding not only dictated preferred behaviour but also a comprehensive view of justice.

Europeans were aware of Mi'kmaq domestic law and called it *habenquedoic*, which they translated as "he did not begin it; he has paid him back; quits and [is] good friends." It is a law of peace, and extends to conduct among other animate creatures. Today this concept is usually referred to as *"mi'kmawey,"* the Mi'kmaq way.

Initiating the customary habenquedoic process was a family responsibility. The offended family had a right to retaliate; the offender's family the duty to refrain from contributing to the disharmony, by not interfering. It must be remembered that there were usually blood relatives on each side of a controversy, however, which facilitated resolution. This was not the direct responsibility of the Mawi'omi or state. The Mi'kmaq did not have any adjudicative institution, no inquisitional system, no specialized professional elite, because they did not conceive of "public" wrongs. There were only private wrongs, and families themselves were the courts. This remains our vision of a fair and equitable justice system.

The imposition of British concepts of coercive order, rights and their quibbling law books, has created fundamental conflicts of the Mi'kmaq social vision. Colonial and racial domination were neither an innocent nor decorous process; they were a process often sanctified as law. The violence of law toward the Mi'kmaq legal inheritance is the hallmark of the colonial period after the signing of the Treaties.

Often these oppressive processes caused and continues to cause a consensus to break down among the Mi'kmaq as they scrambled to survive; yet the deep structure of the Mi'kmaq order, its language, and values have survived. The imposed legal and political concepts of the "civilizing mission" by sheer brute force have not totally disintegrated the cognitive worldview or communion of values and understanding among the Mi'kmaq speakers. Rather, they have only rendered the worldview inarticulate. It is a silence coerced by the force of foreign laws.

Among those who still think and speak in Mi'kmaq language, the distinct and coherent worldview remains operative. Instead of disintegrating the Mi'kmaq order, the imposed values have merely transformed into different sentiments of obligations and accepted practices common to Indigenous society.

Because of the persistence of the racism and colonialism and the "white man's burden," Nova Scotians still assume that the Mi'kmaq and their culture are inferior to British or European civilization. Mi'kmaq have been, and still are presumed to be, at lower stages of development. Canadians arrogantly assume that centuries of oppression have caused Indigenous people to lose their worldview, becoming once again lawless "savages." They do not understand the resiliency of our consciousness.

The lessons to be learned from the Marshall Inquiry are valuable to the Mi'kmaq. The Mi'kmaq have learned that Nova Scotia justice is not neutral; the system has its prejudices and its political intrigues. His Majesty's Law and our view of Nova Scotia justice will no longer be protected by its mythology of fairness. For a short period of time, the Law had replaced our old legends concerned with half-human heroes and tricksters. His Majesty's Law was seen as the culture-hero who protects the tribes from the alien tricksters. Most Mi'kmaq are convinced that they receive public aid because of the Compact and the trust responsibility of the federal government; not because they are needy citizens. Most also believe that only our Aboriginal and Treaty rights stand between them and termination of their limited self-governing status in federal law.

What Nova Scotians did not learn is that success in victimizing a minority emboldens government and endows discriminatory principles of law with a certain aura of precedent and familiarity. The discrimination treatment of unpopular minorities creates dangerous innovation in law. Once accustomed and commonplace, the discrimination principles always seem less cruel and easier to generalize. After a time, there is no longer a minority and majority. The discriminatory exception has become the oppressive rule.

The Grand Council has fought through this concept of the Canadian master race democracy and finally entrenched, again, our Aboriginal and Treaty rights. We have helped clarify our Treaty rights before the highest courts in Nova Scotia and Canada. But still there is a blatant discrepancy between our constitutional rights and, in Nova Scotia, administration of justice. This is another battle that the Mi'kmaq will have to fight. The Marshall Commission was one opportunity to move the administration of justice over Mi'kmaq away from oppression and into the constitutional era.

Recommendations

1. The administration of the Criminal Code on any land which is reserved for the Mi'kmaq should specifically reserve to the tribal courts any specific areas secured to the exclusive jurisdiction of the tribe by Treaty; any intra-Mi'kmaq conflicts, crimes against property and victimless crimes; and the right to preempt provincial procedures and regulation by punishing Mi'kmaq through the law of the tribe, no matter what the offence or against whom; the right to initiate extradition of Mi'kmaq to federal or provincial courts; and the right to have the conflict removed to federal and provincial courts.

2. Significant additional financial and technical assistance from the federal government should be provided to establish, and maintain two tribal courts in Nova Scotia, one on the mainland and another on Cape Breton Island, and for the development of tribal law and order codes. The federal courts should not only supervise tribal courts but also act as the tribal appellate court. Fines should help support the tribal court system.

3. The administration of justice for the Mi'kmaq outside the reserved lands should rest primarily with the federal courts rather than the provincial courts. Provisions should be made in the immediate future that federal courts should have one or two of their staff, a special court workers program and defence attorneys specifically designated with responsibility for Mi'kmaq matters and crimes prosecution on a long-term basis to assure cultural and legal expertise and familiarity.

4. To assist the staff, attorneys and justices of the federal court in becoming sensitive to Mi'kmaq history, Aboriginal and Treaty rights and cultural values, the federal government should allocate sufficient resources so that a mandatory training program and continuing education of the Bar and judges should be administered.

5. The federal and tribal courts should have exclusive criminal jurisdiction over questions of Aboriginal and Treaty rights —especially hunting, fishing, trapping, gathering, and economic rights — as well as Child Welfare and Custody to ensure long-term legal expertise and familiarity.

6. Provision should be made in the immediate future for funds to vindicate Aboriginal and Treaty rights. Federal court rules should include specific legislative provision for the recovery of attorney fees and expenses against any litigant in vindication of an Aboriginal and Treaty right brought by or against a Mi'kmaw, and where the Mi'kmaw prevails in such a suit. Of particular importance are situations where the exercise of rights is frustrated by acts or omissions of the Province.

7. The various federal Crown prosecutors should be required to develop standards for their decision on which cases will be prosecuted and which declined. There should be provision for meaningful tribal participation in all cases specifically requested by the tribe to be prosecuted and such cases should be given priority consideration. In addition, where the Crown declines prosecution, the cases could be immediately referred to the affected tribal court for a determination as to whether it will prosecute under tribal law. Appropriations from Parliament or Treasury Board should designate funds for that purpose.

8. The federal government should allocate sufficient resources so that a comprehensive program of education for non-Natives can be conducted to inform the public about Aboriginal and Treaty rights as the distinguishing feature of Mi'kmaq culture rather than race.

9. To the extent that the federal government may be determined not to have the recommended authority, the federal government should totally fund these recommendations within the provincial adminstration of justice and educational systems.

10. Both the federal government and the Province should cooperatively allocate sufficient resources so that a comprehensive program of Aboriginal and Treaty rights for non-Natives can be conducted to replace the racial standard of differentiation in Nova Scotia; such program should include an evaluation of the history and civics curricula utilized by elementary, secondary, and higher education institutions, the identification of gaps and inaccuracies in such curricula, and the provision of model curricula which accurately reflects Mi'kmaq history, tribal rights, and culture.

Notes

[1] Kjikeptin, or Grand Captain, Alex Denny is a key member of the Santé Mawi'omi Wijit Mi'kmaq, the Grand Council of the Mi'kmaq Nation. These remarks are taken from a speech he gave to the Nova Scotia Barristers' Society in the fall of 1991.

Also from Fernwood Publishing

Feminist Pedagogy
An Autobiographical Approach
Anne-Louise Brookes

Beyond the Limits of the Law
Corporate Crime and Law and Order
John McMullan

Re-Thinking the Administration of Justice
Dawn Currie and Brian MacLean eds.

State Theories
From Liberalism to the Challenge of Feminism
(second edition)
Murray Knuttila

Deconstructing a Nation
Immigration, Multiculturalism and Racism in 90s Canada
Vic Satzewich ed.

The Crisis of Socialist Theory
Strategy and Practice
Joe Roberts ed.

and the Basics from Fernwood...

Issumatuq
Learning from the Tradiitonal Healing Wisdom of the Canadian Inuit
Kit Minor

Man's Will to Hurt
Investigating the Causes, Supports and Varieties of His Violence
Joseph A. Kuypers

Elusive Justice
Beyond the Marshall Inquiry
Joy Mannette ed.